Jenny Huston

In Bloom

IRISH BANDS NOW

Foreword by Glen Hansard

CURRACH
PRESS

FOR JANE: MOTHER, MENTOR, FRIEND

First published in 2009 by
CURRACH PRESS
55A Spruce Avenue,
Stillorgan Industrial Park,
Blackrock, County Dublin
www.currach.ie
1 3 5 4 2

Cover design, page design
and origination by Studio Aad
Cover photograph of The Coronas
at the Olympia Theatre, Dublin
by Dara Munnis
(dara.munnis@gmail.com)

Printed by Gutenberg Press, Malta
ISBN: 978-1-85607-985-3

Acknowledgements

Photographs by: Dara Munnis, Conor Masterson, Richard Gilligan, Enda Doran, Zoran Orlic, Siobhan Quigley, Warren King, Annika Johansson, Pauline Rowan, Roger Bechirian, Tony Kinlan, Jan Von Holloben, Gordon Goodwin, M&E, Graham Keogh, James Minchin III, Ian Moynihan, Daragh Shanahan, Alessio Michelini, Tara McCormack, Justin Moffat, Kev Keogh, Tania Reihll, Enda Casey, Jeannie O'Brien, Noelle Pogue, Loreana Rushe, Gavin Millar, Keith Kiernan, Maura Murphy, Alex Sinclair, Daniel Cooper, John Daly, James Goulden, Graham Smith, Dean Chalkley, Fiona Morgan, Jay Brooks, Stefan Syrowatka.

Transcribing by: Jan Ní Fhlanagáin, Fergal Browne, Sadhbh Connor, Brynmor Pattison, Joseph Orr, Donnacha Coffey, Anna O'Reardon.

A special thank you to Glen Hansard for his foreword and to John Walshe, my second pair of eyes.

Thank you to: Emma Harney, Susan O'Grady, Liza Geddes, Fin O'Leary, Angela Dorgan, Pete Murphy, Aileen Galvin, Orla Breslin, Dan Oggly, Mary-Kate Murphy, Deirdre Crookes, Eddie Brennan, Stevo Berube, Bernie Divilly, Cillian McDonnell, Jeff Robinson, Rory Murphy, Oliver Walsh, Lorcan Ennis, Jim Lawless, Dave O'Grady, Justin Moffatt, Saul Marcus, Ken Allen, Hugh Murray, Niall Muckian, Andrew Ferris, Roger Quail, Claire Leadbitter, Cormac Battle, Dan Hegarty and Jenny Greene (for support over coffees in 2fm), Gerry Ryan and The Gerry Ryan Show team, Ian Wilson, Sinead Troy, Jack Murray, Louise Ni Chriodan, Aoife Woodlock, Zoe Liston, Ingrid Goodwin, Noel Kelly and Niamh Kirwan at NK Management, James Hickey at Matheson Ormsby Prentice, all my lovely friends and family and anyone else who gave me advice or an ear along the way.

Thanks to my editor, Jo O'Donoghue, Gráinne Ross, Cecilia West, Michael Brennan, Patrick O'Donoghue and everyone at Currach Press, and to Scott Burnett, Johnny Kelly and everyone at Studio Aad.

To all the musicians interviewed: thank you for sharing your stories.

FOREWORD BY

Glen Hansard

<u>What is a band?</u> What's it about? A bunch of mates who don't want to be like their folks? Or get a real job? A gang? A bunch of musos who want to perfect their talent? Awkward lads who just want to meet girls but don't want to have to talk to them, or who want to express some unspoken narrative regardless of whether people get it or not? Who want to live in a mansion on Killiney Hill? To change the world? Or is it just about the free drink?

— I think it's all these things.

'Welcome on board! It's great to have you here at Island Records. You know, it really doesn't matter how many records you sell first time out, or second even; we're a career-building label. We'd hope that by album five, you'll be a name people will know and like...so don't feel like you have to knock the doors down with your first record. Take your time: we'll help you work with who you want. Let's walk this road together.'

That was how my first record company meeting went. I was talking to Chris Blackwell, founder of Island Records. I couldn't believe my luck, I floated out of that meeting. I had ascended into the realm of the 'signed', walking the same corridors as Marley, Drake, Waits, Martyn, the Incredible String Band, and, of course, U2, Ireland's giant rock band.

A week later Blackwell stepped out of the job and Island Records became a very different place, at least to me.

The Frames' first record was a difficult one. There were constant battles about choices we made and about what the label wanted 'for us'. They wanted me to write with other songwriters – which kills any confidence you had in the first place. This idea that you're not good enough just as you are is soul-destroying to any young man with hopes and talent. It quickly began to feel as if we were employed. Our first record suffered dreadfully, mostly because it had no direction. Trying to be true to yourself and keep everyone happy produces shit.

Just before our first American tour, Colm, our violin player, had a collapsed lung and was rushed to hospital. He almost died and we decided not to go on the tour without him. A band from Limerick the record company had just signed – the Cranberries – went in our place and had a great tour. The label saw our loyalty to Colm as a weakness and it didn't help our cause.

London seemed to be the centre of operations for most bands: they were signed to English labels or moved to London to record their albums as we did. I'd grown up hating England and the English, not because I was a racist, but because it was all I saw and heard as a kid growing up in Dublin. It was in the air, it was in the songs, it was spoken about around dinner tables. We went on the hunger strike marches [in 1981]; we wore black armbands when the hunger strikers died; we

IN BLOOM - FOREWORD

sprayed BRITS OUT everywhere we could. It was only as I grew up that I questioned these beliefs and came up with different answers, but still, for an Irish guy with all that prejudice in his formative years to have to travel to London every few weeks hoping to get some money to tour or to make a new demo, or try to convince some guy in a suit that I was worthy of his writing a cheque for me – it all felt like going to the dole office and the dole in Ireland was a lot easier to deal with.

When our first record was finished and printed and pressed I went for a meeting at the Island offices with our manager (the father of my girlfriend at the time); we were to talk about touring and so on. The result was that the Island man threw the tape across the room at me and told me what a pile of shit he thought it was and how he hated Irish bands; especially us. We stood up and left. It took all our strength not to run back in and tear the arrogant fucker's head off. That was the end of that...

Being 'dropped' is a difficult thing to go through, no matter what way you justify it. It killed me that I'd let myself get pushed around during the recording and that we'd made a record that didn't do anyone involved any justice. I blamed myself and at the same time knew I was the only one who was going to get myself out of it. After the whining, you grow up: we wrote some of the best tunes we'd written thus far. There was a lot of 'Fuck you!' in the songs: so what doesn't kill you makes you angry and focused. We started making demos for our next record; we borrowed money from our families to rehearse; we chipped in half our dole to pay for the rehearsal room. We were a band and looking for another deal (idiots). The definition of insanity: 'Making the same mistake twice, expecting a different outcome.' It's said that the two most ripped-off professions are musicians and boxers and it's because they just want to get into the ring and fight! And they'll do anything for that, for the sound of applause.

I met Donal Dineen in Bewleys one evening in 1993 or 1994 and he passionately and clearly made a great argument for the Frames not seeking a label: he suggested we create our own. This was our introduction to the idea of DIY. Donal's plan for us was: we'd record this song we had – 'Revelate' – with money borrowed from Whelans bar, in advance of a gig we'd play for them later. Our friend Donal Scannell would make us a video for nothing (£2 for the VHS tape); we would put the VHS into security cameras around Dublin and I'd mime the tune into the cameras. We'd take out the tape and there you have it...a video.

At the time, Donal Dineen was presenting *No Disco*, a breakthrough show on RTÉ that featured pretty much anything Donal wanted to play. He played our video and everything began to shift for us. Our single sold well and we used the money to start recording our next album, *Fitzcarraldo*. This time was the birth of a whole new era in Irish music: Donal would play videos by bands from all over the country; all they had to do was send one in. Suddenly there were bands coming out of the woodwork all over Ireland – great bands! Plus Donal changed live gigs; he would announce tours by the bands on the show and suddenly the gigs were full. Before that, during the rave era, bands would 'open up' for the DJ. You'd have an empty room at the start of your set and by the end the room might be full, but with only a few dedicated followers of the band listening and a few hundred people totally ignoring us. Then we'd finish our set and as we took down the gear, the floor would fill with dancers for the DJ set.

With *No Disco*, suddenly everyone felt they were part of something, it was a unifying force in Ireland and it gave a voice to anyone who had one. The DJ slot continued but on a more even playing field. Although we did make the same mistake again and lived through it again, we were never the same after that first chat with

Donal. A door had opened, an idea seeded. We started Plateau records with Claire, our friend and new manager who had left her job at the label we were signed to (ZTT), because she had just stopped believing in it. All a manager is is a mate who would lie down in the middle of the road for your band. If you have a mate like that, that's your manager. You don't need experience; that comes. You just need to believe in the tunes and the people playing them.

The one great thing that's been a constant through the Frames' lifetime is that we had an audience. People would come out and see us when we played, which is the most empowering thing for any band. If you have patrons you can continue to make your music without the need for great reviews in press or TV appearances. Touring Ireland continuously not only got us off the dole but helped us to tour the States, helped us to make records. No, it didn't just help, it completely financed the existence of the Frames. It became obvious to us that if we kept a clear and honest relationship with our audience, not taking anything for granted and treating people with respect, we could achieve anything.

We set up licensing deals in different countries and had our records reaching far and wide through a bunch of small labels around the world: guys in their bedroom who distributed a few records they liked. This felt like the best way to stay in touch with what was going out and how it was selling. The numbers were super-modest but it was a start.

We recorded For the Birds between a house in Kerry and Steve Albini's studio in Chicago. This was a new chapter for us again: Steve was great with his advice and time. We got a deal with a small label, Overcoat, distributed through Touch and Go in Chicago. A friend of Steve's, Howard Greynolds, put out our records and became our US manager also (he still is) and we've all grown together through these experiences. We were in control of our destiny and that is the best feeling in the world. It struck me that all the good things that happened in our career had come from us. They hadn't come from some big label boss or super manager; it was by our own effort. So every inch we gained, we felt satisfied we'd earned it.

In the early days of the Frames we couldn't get a word mentioned about us on radio or in any music press in Ireland, which was frustrating, yet we continued to tour and build our audience, until eventually our audience was big enough that we had at least to be acknowledged. This felt like a success. Irish music journalism for the longest time was chiefly concerned with 'cool', which usually meant English or English-sounding. This laziness was rampant. It seemed somehow really 'uncool' to be an Irish band in the British music press and, astonishingly, it was the same here at home. It wasn't until Donal's years at No Disco that rural Ireland had its voice.

Things are different now in many ways but in many ways not. People still sign to English labels, go through the heartache of being dropped and signed and dropped again, but that's all part of the learning. I wouldn't change a thing on the road we've come...

There's a different soul to what we do in Ireland, I don't think Irish bands have ever really been 'cool'. Cool is a French thing, a London thing, a New York thing; the Irish have too many conflicting emotions to sustain 'cool'. We don't feel comfortable in shades, we have something else, something great, something complex and elemental. We're far too self-aware to think only about the exterior. I don't think Irish people are better – just different – and that gives us something.

This is not just our story but the story of a lot of bands. Some in this book are friends we've known through the years. Some stuck with it and others fell by the wayside or got so cynical they just stopped believing in the fight. What makes one band 'make it' and another not has nothing to do with talent. It's all about willpower and keeping your nerve. One band's version of success is in total contrast to another's. Someone said, 'The luckiest people I've known coincidentally also happen to be the hardest working.' There's something in that . Sometimes you just have to take the attitude: 'I know what I'm doing and I know it'll all make sense one day. There's some pattern to it all and I can't quite see it or verbalise it, but I just know I'll have my time.'

When we made *Once* with John Carney there was no way of knowing then that this film would be the thing that would open a door to a whole other level of success for myself and Marketa and the Frames, and it couldn't have come at a better time. And it surely proves the point, at least to me, that if you set out on a road with a clear idea of where you're going, no matter how many cul de sacs or wrong turns you walk down, you'll always right yourself and not waste time moving towards your goal, whatever that is for you. As someone wiser than me once said, 'Success is not a destination, it's a way of travelling...'

On we go.

Strict Joy by the Swell Season is out now on Plateau: **www. theswellseason.com**.

Jenny Huston

THE MUSIC BUSINESS IS A CRUEL
AND SHALLOW MONEY TRENCH,
A LONG PLASTIC HALLWAY WHERE
THIEVES AND PIMPS RUN FREE, AND
GOOD MEN DIE LIKE DOGS. THERE'S
ALSO A NEGATIVE SIDE.

HUNTER S. THOMSON

I came to Ireland in 1996, having spent my teenage and college years in Victoria, Canada. Seattle was only hours away and grunge was the soundtrack. I arrived in Kilkenny, obsessed with alternative rock and indie pop, to discover a vibrant band scene full of like-minded people. I felt at home.

It wasn't long before I got involved in music here, volunteering to DJ at the local radio station – absorbing and sharing all I could. Music is my passion and my desire to shout about it remains as strong as ever.

It was apparent then that U2 had set the bar very high for bands in this country, something that is still true today. Their level of commercial success is so extraordinary, in global terms, that it is virtually unattainable for other bands. Although it is not a fair benchmark, this benchmark exists, and consequently few Irish bands are sufficiently praised for their successes inside or outside Ireland.

When you remove U2 from the equation (and other artists that have a book of their own to reflect their career) and take a really current look at successful Irish bands, you are left with a remarkably large selection. This book is a snapshot of these artists, a look at some of the new headline bands, those that have come to prominence since 2000: bands whose careers are in full bloom. Irish bands now.

This is not a list or an A-Z of Irish bands. It does not cover all genres or give a critical analysis of a band's work. It is a celebration of some of the artists who are in our charts, played on our radio stations and filling venues around the country.

Many of these bands have impressive international stories, with album releases and huge followings in other countries. They have achieved a great deal of their success by themselves. Many have done so by means of their own labels, with their own money, through blood, sweat, tears and perseverance. These were the stories I wanted to tell.

As a music lover, someone in awe of their talent, I wanted to get a better understanding of how these band members became musicians; how their talent was nurtured; how they got where they are. I had the same list of guide interview questions for everyone: simple questions, that led to the most diverse of answers. How did it all start? Did they take music lessons as children? Were they from musical families? Where was their first gig? When was their first headline show? How do they make it work on a practical/business level? Were there any major struggles along the way? Any advice? Success is defined is many different ways: what is success for them? What were the highlights so far?

It's not a secret that the music industry is in crisis. Record labels are downsizing, merging, being bought over and going bankrupt. The industry has been dramatically and permanently changed by technology. Access to music has never been better. Getting your music heard has never been simpler. Being paid for the music you make has never been harder. The online world of downloads, file sharing and streaming has created numerous challenges for creative artists and the companies that seek to profit from their work. It is an interesting time for musicians.

Record labels no longer have money to spend on development. Bands are being dropped when they don't go platinum on their first album or when they fail to make money for the label. Labels are businesses after all, there to make money, but very few of the legends we celebrate today – think of Joni Mitchell, Neil Young, Bob Dylan, Leonard Cohen, even Radiohead – would ever have become legends if they were subject to the current industry conditions: 'I don't hear daytime radio. Go back and write more singles... Call the stylist!'

Thankfully, Ireland has a proud DIY tradition brought to prominence in the 1990s by The Frames. Hundreds of Irish bands now self-release each year.

But recording and releasing is only half the battle. Keeping a band together is often the biggest challenge. Longevity is rare and something to be admired in a band and it is with sadness that we've seen bands split up or wind up. All the artists featured in this book have shown massive personal commitment to their music, whether they are signed to a major label or an independent label or are self-released.

Everyone has been extremely generous in sharing their stories, telling me about the high points of their careers as well as the low. The artists' honesty about the challenges and pressures of the industry will be invaluable to those hoping to follow them and learn from them: the stresses of major label deals; the perils and necessities of contracts; the advantages of staying involved in the day-to-day; learning to trust your instincts (other people don't always know best for you); the need for time and space to develop your sound; the creative freedom that is essential, not optional.

To those who are starting out on the same path: don't be discouraged, dream the big dream. Play in your bedroom, play with friends. Do the work. Sing, create, experiment. Find your sound. Get out there.

The path is paved. Eager ears are waiting.

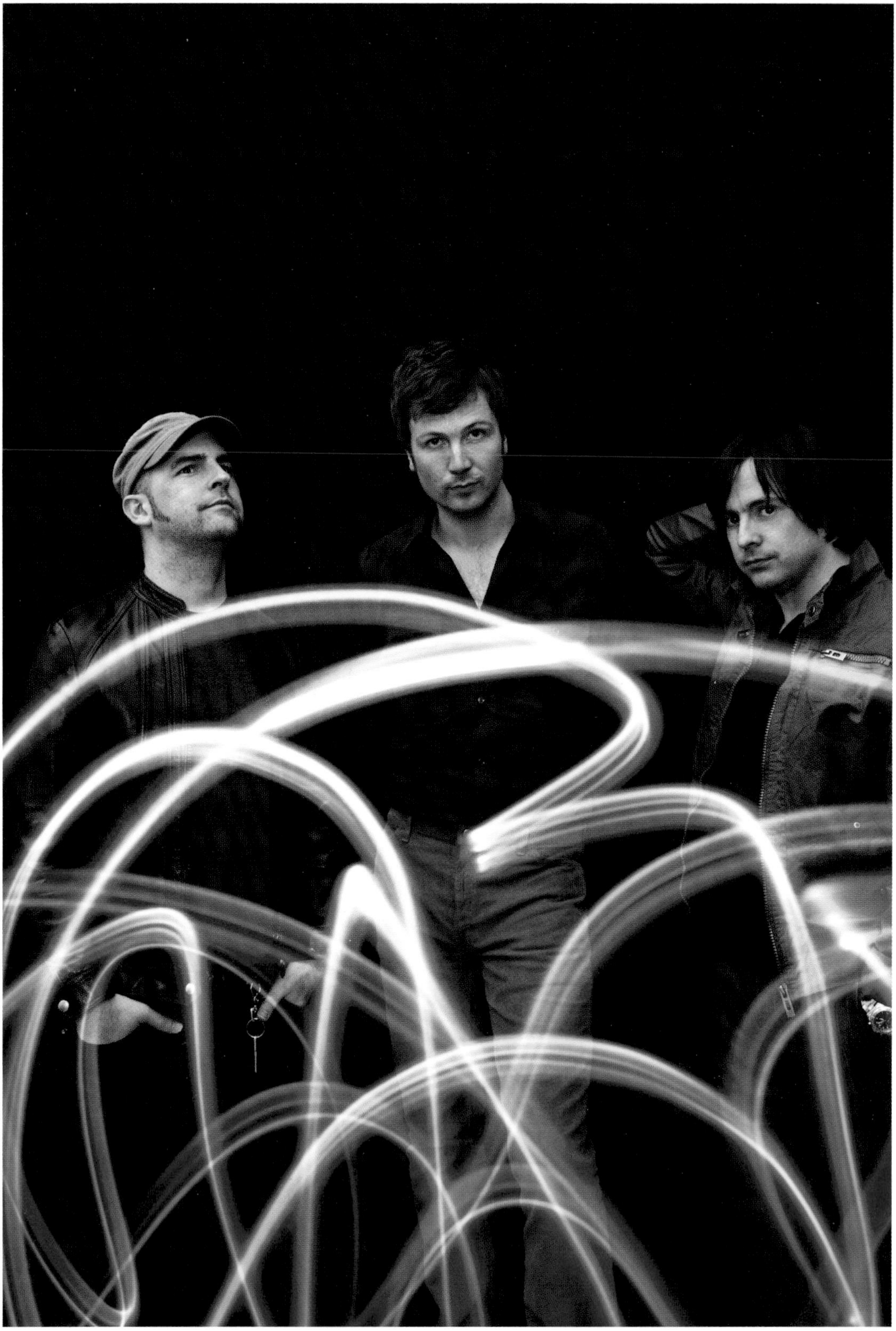

© JAN VON HOLLEBEN

Bell X1

Band Members
Paul Noonan
Dominic Phillips
David Geraghty

Albums
Neither Am I

Music in Mouth

Flock

Tour De Flock – Live at the Point

Blue Lights on the Runway

Label
BellyUp Records

Management
Roger Bechirian, Trick Management

Co-Management
North America
Foye Johnson, Intrigue Group

Websites
www.bellx1.com

www.myspace.com/bellx1

Bell X1 are intelligent, creative, gifted musicians and the band is one of the most successful and best-loved in the country. When they are together they joke, slag and finish each other's sentences, making it great fun to watch them bounce off each other.

Paul's intelligence lends itself to quick humour and mischief. Far from the intense, serious, front man picture some journalists have painted him (overly serious people don't write about Cornetto ice cream and picking at your knickers), Paul is funny. He is a great storyteller and a genuinely lovely guy, as goofy and silly as he is thoughtful and reflective.

Dave is the messer. He has a funny aside for almost everything said, yet is completely focused and passionate about music. Dom has an easygoing likeability, striking you as exactly the sort of person you would like to be stuck on a tour bus with: interesting, good-natured and fun.

Bell X1 have enjoyed multi-platinum success, including the Number 1 albums *Flock* and *Blue Lights on the Runway*. They have numerous Meteor Awards nominations, including Best Irish Live Performance and Best Irish Band, and were shortlisted for the inaugural Choice Music Prize Irish Album of the Year for *Flock* in 2005. 'The Great Defector' spent so many weeks at Number 1 in the airplay charts that it kept U2 from the top spot, also proving a huge radio hit in North America, being playlisted on radio stations from New York to Vancouver.

Bell X1's extensive touring has brought them to festivals like Oxegen, Electric Picnic, T in the Park, the Great Escape, Benicassim, Hop Farm and Austin City Limits, while they have also headlined their own shows in the RDS, the Point, Malahide Castle and the Marquee in Cork.

DOM, PAUL AND DAVE WERE PRESENT FOR THE INTERVIEW. BRIAN CROSBY WAS SUBSEQUENTLY INTERVIEWED.

They have performed on David Letterman's *Late Show* (twice: the first time with 'Rocky Took A Lover'; the second time with 'The Great Defector'), *The Tonight Show* with Conan O'Brien, Craig Ferguson's *The Late Late Show* and numerous other high-profile American and Canadian TV shows, while their music has been used in *Grey's Anatomy*, *The OC*, *Teachers* and *One Tree Hill*.

Their history is a long one. Dominic Phillips, Paul Noonan, Brian Crosby and Damien Rice were all in the same class in secondary school in Celbridge, County Kildare. 'We all knew one another but we weren't best mates,' admits Dom. 'At the end of school there was a folk group, music for Masses and things that were on: it was really an excuse to get out of class so you could practise. That's how we initially started playing together.'

It was in college, however, that the four really gelled. By pure coincidence, the entire quartet studied Engineering at Trinity College, where they became good friends during their first year.

'Damien dropped out after the first year and he used to play pub gigs and that kind of thing,' recalls Dom. 'Then that went into different avenues where he would play with himself and Brian as a two-piece or he'd play just on his own. Brian didn't want to do so many gigs, so myself and Paul would play with him. Then it just got a bit more serious and we started writing some songs.'

Paul, Dom and Brian went to America for the summer on a J1 and Damien continued playing in Dublin with his girlfriend at the time, through whom he met Dave.

Dave recalls: 'When I met the lads, they had recorded a demo called *The J-plane* and I wasn't blown away by it but I thought, "These lads are serious. They've made a demo, and it sounds like they're serious." So I went: "Right, I'll jump aboard with these lads and see what happens." And fifteen years later, it's still happening.'

The other four had an understanding with their parents that they'd finish college before really concentrating on the band. The band was called Juniper. During their last year, they found a big house in the country, which became their home, their base of operations and their studio.

Dom confesses that he thought of it more of a pastime, just hanging out with the lads: 'I remember thinking, a lot of people go travelling for a year so we'll probably give it a year and see how it goes. I never thought it would go anywhere, if I'm honest.'

'Thanks, Dom,' laughs Paul.

Their first gig may have been an eighteenth birthday party that included loads of cover versions but it wasn't long before their own material was on show. After the summer, they started playing in the Da Club in Dublin, including a residency for the month of November: 'We'd make the journey into town to do the big show,' smiles Paul.

'Bringing our gear in a horse box,' interjects Dave.

'Yeah, we had a horse box,' laughs Paul.

'There was something really cool about the Da Club at that time. It had an almost speakeasy sort of vibe and it was packed. There was this guy called Tim Kirby who used to run it, who was a former Iron Maiden roadie and he used to make a little speech before every act and then with a little flourish he would say, "This is your stage," and the band would come on,' recalls Paul, with a grin.

'There was a community feeling about it,' he continues. 'Doing a residency there, I felt that we built up a fan base made up of people we didn't actually know. Because when you start playing, it's usually people you know, family and friends, who are being supportive and come in. You reach a point where you realise that people you don't know are coming to see you and it's a great milestone.'

Dom agrees. 'That's when you start taking it a bit more seriously. We did four or five band bashes in the Rock Garden and you're given forty tickets per band and you have to get rid of them and

if you don't sell them, you have to pay for them, basically, so you're asking friends to supplement the show. It's exciting to play initially but it soon becomes, "I don't want to be doing *that*." You've got to play for people you don't know.'

They might not have been paid very much but there was a reward for sold-out shows. 'One of Tim's grand flourishes was that he'd have champagne in the dressing room afterwards,' remembers Paul. 'He had this tiny room and if it was full, he'd do the champagne.'

Things started to step up a gear for Juniper: 'We got management early the next year and I remember one day the manager saying to us, "Our objective is to have you signed by Christmas." That was one of the first times that I went, "Oh right, so that'd be a plan," because before that, we had just been meandering,' reckons Dom.

Their management fine-tuned the line-up and went after a record deal: 'Paul and Damien and I all sing, so we used to swap instruments before we got management,' explains Dave. 'They came in and went, "*He*'s [Damien] the singer," and we all had our roles then.'

'They brought a few people out to listen to us in the house. We had one room where we had the gear set up all the time and someone would come in and listen to us play five or six songs and nod and rub their chin,' laughs Dom.

'We used to do these insane buffets of food,' recalls Paul, with a grin. 'We'd have sandwiches, cake and tea in the kitchen.'

Juniper finally signed to PolyGram Ireland: 'I remember we had a signing party at La Stampa on Dawson Street and invitations went out with this little drawing of the Polygram office and it said, "Polygram Ireland welcomes Juniper to the home of the hits,"'groans Paul. 'It was all very

"Smashie and Nicey". It was a new world for us. We very much left the business side of things to the management and we were kind of dizzy in the first throes of being a band and playing music and having people coming to your shows; it was very exciting.'

'The deal we had with them was for three singles followed by six albums, in theory. You did your first single and then they would pick up the option for the second single if they wanted it. We did two singles and we were to do a third single with the album and then Damien decided he didn't want to do the album,' explains Dom.

Damien Rice left before the album was recorded and later started an internationally successful solo career on his own label.

'He obviously felt the band was pulling in a different direction from where he wanted to go and things were out of his control; things were being done that he didn't agree with,' recalls Dave. 'He wanted to be his own man and make his own decisions without having to confer with band members, which is fair enough. For him, he made the right decision and for us as well. We've gone our separate ways and we fit our own niches that we've made ourselves.'

'The reality is, if somebody stamps their feet on a particular issue they'll probably get their way,' notes Dom, 'but I think in Damien's case, he is not of that mindset. He was much happier to be in control of everything, I suppose.'

'We went for a pint in Celbridge,' Dave remembers. 'The four of us sat there and we were like, "What are we gonna do, are we gonna continue?" We just said, "Yeah, we'll continue, Paul's the singer," and we started writing songs in Celbridge GAA.'

'Effectively we went to PolyGram and said, "Damien is leaving; we'd like to continue,"' explains Dom. 'Jim O'Neill [Finance Director in PolyGram] was very supportive and he said, "Go and record some demos and let's have a look and see." And we did: we spent about three months doing up an eight-track demo.'

At the same time, their management company left them. 'They had put so much time and their own money in, so the bubble burst for them,' Dave recalls. 'So we had all these songs and

IN BLOOM - BELL X1

it was time to come up with a name to put on the CD we were giving to the record company, so we spent three days trawling books and magazines just trying to come up with an idea for a new name.

'We came across a *Guinness Book of Records*,' he continues. 'It had a hundred years in the book, so each page was encapsulated. 1964, I think it was: the Bell X-1 [A US Air Force research aircraft] broke the sound barrier. We were all sitting round at this stage, just going fucking mad: we were like addicts, hooked on books, and Dom said "What about Bell X1? Write it down!"' laughs Dave, remembering the process.

The band had written pages of options for their new name. Names like Datsun and Interpol were considered: 'We'd just read out of the list and somebody would go, "No!" laughs Dom.

'It was the downside to the democratic process,' grins Paul.

And so Bell X1 was born.

'When we recorded this eight-track demo it was the four of us, without Damien and without management, and for me, that's when we became what we are now,' reflects Dom. 'In one way, it was a great thing because even though we were still in a major label tie, it meant we were now taking responsibility for ourselves: between the four of us, everyone tended to gravitate towards whatever aspect they liked to do and then everything was covered.'

Self-management can be both liberating and daunting: 'Brian and I went into meetings in Universal feeling a little under-dressed and in over our heads,' admits Paul.

The label loved the demos and Bell X1 recorded the first album *Neither Am I* with Universal Music Ireland (their contract was moved to the Universal Music Group with the buy-out of PolyGram by Seagram in 1998). It was recorded in a residential studio in Wales and produced by Nick Seymour from Crowded House.

'That was really exciting,' remembers Dom. 'You were living there, you were in the studio, you were making an album: you were living the dream.'

'It was great to have an album because with Juniper we never got to make an album. It always felt a little unfinished. A little "fur coat and no knickers",' jokes Paul. 'We'd had two very high-profile singles and no album to follow it and it felt a little hollow, I suppose. Whereas, with this, we had an album that felt like a substantial body of work and we liked the idea of having an album that had some sort of theme or had a coherent aesthetic. Not that it particularly had!'

For their second album, *Music in Mouth*, Bell X1 moved their deal to Island Records in London. It was essentially still Universal Records but the new home came with greater credibility [U2, PJ Harvey, Bob Marley, Nick Drake] and resources. The move was instigated by their new manager, Roger Bechirian, whom they had met through Tom McRae. 'We were dealing with different people and they had direct contact with us and we had an A&R [Artist and Repertoire] guy for the first time,' explains Paul. 'It felt more substantial.'

Bell X1 rented a house in Wexford and rehearsed and did pre-production for *Music in Mouth*. The record was done with producer Jamie Cullum in Ridge Farms in Surrey and the Fallout Shelter, London [in the basement of Island Records]. 'The A&R guy would come down every few days and say hello and they'd listen but never really interfere,' recalls Dom.

Music and Mouth did extremely well in Ireland, being full of singles, including the massive 'Eve, The Apple Of My Eye', 'Next To You' and 'Alphabet Soup'. Bell X1 were playing nice venues at home and were given the chance to tour outside Ireland: 'We did the toilets,' quips Dave. (A toilet tour is any number of small venues across the UK that every band starts on: hard work, not very glamorous and some of the venues are kips, hence the name.)

'We did a great tour with Tom McRae,' says Paul 'We did about ten shows in France. Dave and I did an acoustic tour of it once and then we did a full band tour, which was great. It made us very determined to get records out in Europe, which happened with *Flock*.'

Their third album, *Flock,* was recorded in Dublin in Westland Studios by longtime live-sound engineer, Phil Hayes, and produced by the band's manager, Roger. It entered the Irish charts at Number 1. Things were great for the Bellies. '*Flame*' was an instant radio hit, and 'Rocky Took a Lover' was gigantic.

'We recorded "Rocky" in Westland but previous to *Flock*, for a B-side session for *Music in Mouth*. We had a day left so we lashed it down and it was like, "Oh, that's good!" Then we kept it for the record,' explains Dom.

'Rocky' may have been done quickly and intended for a B-side but it was their biggest radio hit to date. Tours and high-profile supports followed, including a UK tour with Keane, followed by a European tour with Starsailor and others.

Bell X1 parted ways with Universal Island after *Flock*. The band was getting excellent reactions on support tours in Europe and selling out self-organised gigs in America but their label wasn't interested in spending the money to follow it up.

'They were London-based, so basically they would have to pay for us to tour elsewhere,' explains Dom. 'If we were touring in France, it wouldn't be Universal France who'd pay for it, it'd still be Island in London. They couldn't justify spending for us to tour in Europe, when we weren't

recouping for them in their own patch. We were getting a bit of a following but it wasn't reaching any sort of tipping point, so that meant that we were stuck wanting to tour outside the UK and not being able to, because we couldn't afford it ourselves and they weren't willing to pay for it.'

'Unfortunately, we fell into the 98 per cent of the experiences of bands with major labels where it's down to the banana-selling mentality,' explains Dave. 'For example, the guy who was plugging us in radio wasn't a fan of the band and they wouldn't pay for outside radio production: shit like that. It was symptomatic of being part of a machine that's fundamentally flawed.'

'The reality was that time was drawing close to making another record and they [the record label] were prepared to make another record but they were obviously not as committed to it and purse strings were going to tighten. So it seemed like a no-brainer to say, "No thanks,"' explains Dom

Bell X1 formed their own label, BellyUp Records, whose first release was the live CD/ DVD set *Tour De Flock* in 2007.

'I think a lot has changed in terms of why bands need labels,' reflects Paul. 'We didn't need a label to make a record: we didn't need a record label to put it out. So we felt it was better just to find some other partners and own the record ourselves.'

Dave agrees. 'The machine might not be as big but at least the cogs turn.'

Bell X1 organised a release of *Flock* in America in 2008. It was a complicated licensing deal where Universal still owned the record but it was put out through a small label in North Carolina called Yep Roc (the same label that had put out Brian's charity record for Oxfam, *The Cake Sale*). It gave Bell X1 a reason to tour extensively and later it would give them a platform from which to continue with the new record.

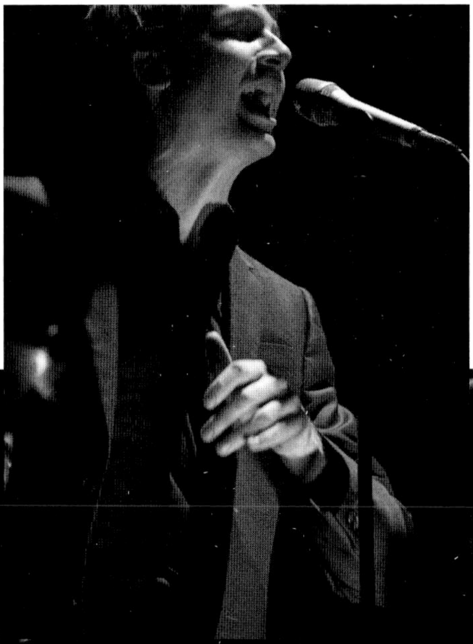

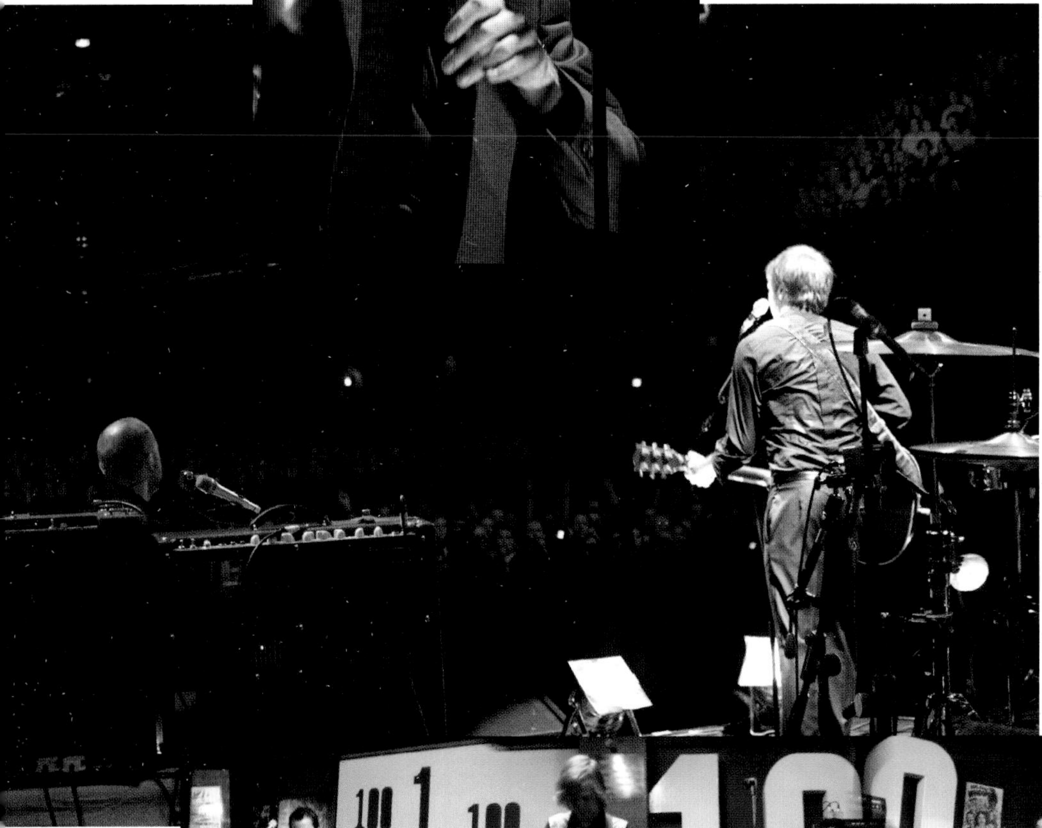

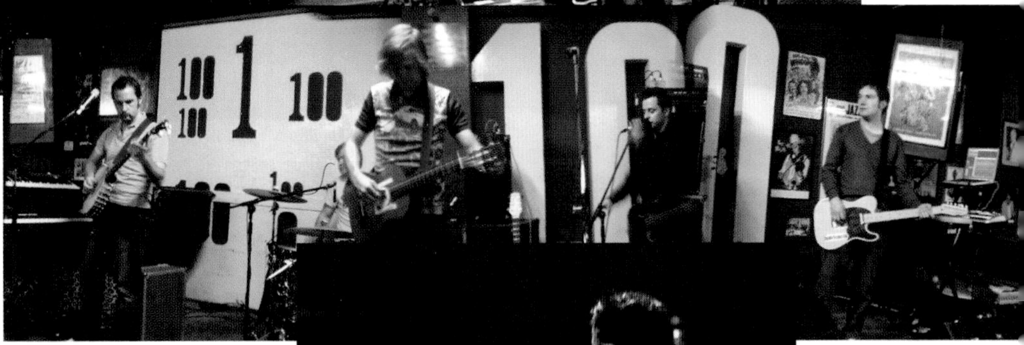
100
100
1
100

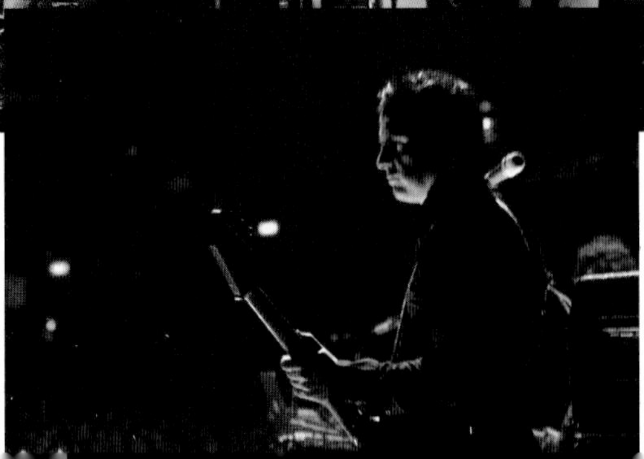

Founding member Brian Crosby announced his intention of leaving the band in 2008, towards the end of the *Flock* campaign. He continued to tour with Bell X1 as normal but did not record any of the new material in non-touring time. The transition was well thought out: designed to cause as little disruption as possible.

'It was partly a time-of-life decision, partly because I had been quite busy doing various other projects, both in producing and because I was getting involved in writing music for pictures, and I really wanted to do more of that,' explains Brian. 'It got to the point where I suppose something had to give. I couldn't commit because a Bell X1 record takes a chunk of time in the studio and I just felt I didn't have it in me to continue committing all that time,' explains Brian.

'I can't remember exactly when I said it but it was about a year and a half before I officially left that I floated my intentions. At that point, I was very busy with other projects and I said I didn't want to record another album. I continued touring with Bell X1 more or less until the new record was coming out, so they were making the new record as I was touring with them, yet I had nothing to do with it. I guess the window was left open on both our parts – we did leave it open for a while – but when it came to the stage where things had to be implemented for Bell X1 to move forward, we solidified the decision.'

'It's really not something that blew up: it just ran its course,' he continues. 'For me, it just came to an end, the guys continue and everyone's doing great. I think first and foremost the guys in the band are my best mates and still are. I wish every success and happiness to them, really genuinely.'

Having had months to reflect since leaving the band, Brian has the necessary distance to look back at all the many highlights for him and for Bell X1 during the time of the first three albums.

'I remember a huge buzz was touring outside Ireland for the first time and certainly when we toured in America for the first time – that was a real feeling of having reached some landmark position. Landing in JFK the first time we arrived in America, arriving there with your band, it feels almost like a filmic moment!' laughs Brian.

'Any time we toured or got to a new country, that was a huge buzz for me. I love travelling; so being able to travel – do shows, eat food, meet people – I got the biggest kick out of that. Definitely, there were a few significant home shows that we did in Ireland. I can look back at all of them from when we first sold out Whelans to when we first played the Point – they were all kind of landmark times, there was a sense of achievement.'

Playing the Point was a once-in-a-lifetime opportunity for the band because a few months later, it was shut down to reopen later on as The O2. 'It was definitely a moment we knew wouldn't happen again,' recalls Brian.

'I remember in the dressing room beforehand, there was a lot of pacing around and it was quite an unnerving gig because we were shooting it for a DVD too – it was kind of a double whammy! Before we went on stage, we were told that the only other Irish bands that had played the Point were U2, Snow Patrol, the Frames…so there was definitely a feeling of being in the VIP club for a while,' he laughs.

Bell X1 are so low-key about their success that one wonders if they celebrate or just take stock after a big moment for the band: 'We generally did celebrate. After every show, there's an after-show party if it's something significant,' says Brian, thinking back on the Point show and the Malahide Castle gig. 'We always marked it in the way most bands do if they're touring, having a drink at the bar afterwards. It's only in situations like this, when you're answering questions on a fifteen-year span or whatever it was, that you recognise that there were quite a few significant moments.'

'It was especially lovely after the first time (the only time!) I did Conan O'Brien. We did the show (you do it during the daytime and it's broadcast that night) and then we went to an Irish bar and we were all trying to stay up, fighting the jet lag.

And we just had pints in our hands and watched ourselves on Conan, which was kind of cool,' says Brian, smiling.

He seems happy knowing he left the band on a high: 'It really was up and running: we were touring a lot the last year I was in Bell X1. I think we had gone to the States four times to do tours; we had seen a lot of the country. We had toured Europe a couple of times and of course we had all these shows in Ireland.'

As to what he is doing now: is he a producer or a musician? 'I'm a musician first. I compose, I produce and I also run a publishing label, so I have all these various bits. I'm spending half my time writing and composing for films, doing soundtracks, then producing with other bands, writing with other people – I love creating music like that.'

Following Tim O'Donovan [Neosupervital] and Brian Crosby's departure, Bell X1 introduced Rory Doyle on drums and Mark Aubele on keys for their live shows. 2009 was a very busy year, with Irish, American and European tours to launch the new album.

Blue Lights on the Runway came out worldwide in March 2009. It's been exceptionally positive for the band. 'We've licensed it in America and in the Benelux [Belgium, the Netherlands and Luxembourg] and we have distribution deals everywhere else,' explains Paul.

The lead single 'The Great Defector' was a massive radio hit, going to Number 1 in the airplay charts and ruling the charts for weeks. Bell X1 were invited to support U2 at one of their Croke Park gigs in July and played Hop Farm, Benicassim and Electric Picnic. The summer season was followed by further, more extensive, touring in the United States and Canada, alongside a host of Irish and European dates.

'I feel It's working for the first time in Europe. We have a foothold in Germany and Poland and places like that. You get the odd Paddy shouting "Setanta Hotel, Celbridge,"' jokes Paul 'but it's not dominant. And things have built steadily in America.'

It's a bit of an understatement but then that's Bell X1 for you. For all their talent and success, they are eternally humble.

The Blizzards

Band Members
Niall Breslin (Bresy)
Justin Ryan
Declan Murphy (Dec)
Aidan Lynch (Lynchie)
Anthony Doran

Albums
A Public Display of Affection
Domino Effect

Label
Universal Music Ireland

Manager
Justin Moffatt (Moff)

Websites
www.theblizzards.ie
www.myspace.com/theblizzards

NIALL BRESLIN REPRESENTED THE BLIZZARDS FOR THE INTERVIEW.

Niall 'Bresy' Breslin makes a big impression. It's not just his physical appearance, which at a muscular 6'6" is more in keeping with a professional athlete than a lead singer – it's his focus that strikes you. He has combined his passion for music and a love of writing with a clear business head. He is the polite, determined antithesis of the flaky rock star.

The Blizzards have amassed a huge following with their ska-pop sound and energetic live shows. They have worked hard to be the excellent live band they are today, gigging up and down the country, playing all the venues and college events on offer. Their début album, *A Public Display of Affection,* spawned numerous hit singles, received massive radio play and catapulted the band into public consciousness. It also achieved platinum record sales. In 2008, *Domino Effect* continued the trend with another string of hits, including, 'Trust Me I'm A Doctor', 'The Reason' and 'Postcards', cementing the Blizzards' position as one of the biggest bands in the country.

A good attitude, radio hits, live energy and business acumen have put the Blizzards on top. They have been nominated for five Meteor Awards (Best Irish Band, Best Irish Pop Act x2, Best Irish Live Performance x2) winning Best Irish Live Performance in 2009. They have supported AC/DC, Kasabian, Kaiser Chiefs, Oasis and the Prodigy, headlined the Academy and the Ambassador Theatre and played Oxegen on numerous occasions.

The Blizzards are of the few successful bands that remain on a major label in Ireland: they have remained on Universal since the beginning. 'Bresy' explains how they made it work. 'When we got signed we said, "That was the easy part and now it really has to kick in." I went in to every meeting to show that I really cared. Anything they asked us to do, even if it was a promo in north Donegal on a Monday morning, we did it. We didn't complain and we earned respect from them and we respected them.'

Many bands have felt that they were pushed towards a more commercial daytime radio sound when they were signed to a major label – the classic 'I want to hear more singles!' – but Bresy says it isn't like that for him: creatively he is doing what he enjoys. 'I love writing pop music; they never made me write pop music. I know a couple of people have come up to me and said our first couple of EPs are really left of centre and different but I got bored with it very easily, I didn't enjoy performing it live and nobody liked it!' he laughs. 'I know I'm a pop merchant, that's what I love.'

One gets the feeling that Bresy and the Blizzards have had to defend their major label status on more than one occasion on an island full of independent bands with a more alternative aesthetic.

'You have to apologise sometimes, because there are thousands of people in this country waiting for the new Arcade Fire to come along. They're realising the biggest issue is that acts aren't allowed to be developed. I mean you look at Radiohead's first record – from a songwriting perspective some of it was poor. We met Tony Visconti, David Bowie's producer, and he said he laughed at everything he was sent for two years by Bowie but Bowie developed and developed.'

Bresy mourns the loss of the front man and not because he doesn't think they are out there. Quite the opposite: he suspects they have been replaced by something less time-consuming – huge backing tracks. 'The art of the front man is dead, it's gone, they don't care about front men any more. How many bands have come out in the last five years and you would wear a T-shirt with their front man on it? You know, iconic, because it's not seen as important. It's gone. Becoming a front man takes a long time.'

Many bands are signed by record labels in bidding wars before they have reached their full potential, only to be dropped before they write their best work. They are no longer given the space to grow and develop they were in the 1970s, 1980s and 1990s: if the album doesn't sell the number of copies the label expects it to (if the label doesn't recoup its expenditure), they are dropped, regardless of relative or critical success.

Bresy is very aware of that reality.

'In Ireland it's all about selling records. If you put five stars from twenty critics up on their desk they don't care: it has to sell. And in this day and age, from our perspective, what we've realised and why we've never gone "licking arse" essentially – we've realised critics don't sell records. In Ireland they don't, people actually rebel against good reviews.'

The Blizzards signed a domestic deal with Universal Ireland. One wonders why, living in a country with a strong DIY ethic, they chose to sign a record deal and whether it was important for them in getting to where they are today. Bresy explains: 'We would never have got Michael Beinhorn to produce an album if we weren't signed. Meeting Beinhorn changed me totally as a musician. Secondly, it gave the band a little bit of confidence when we needed it and it is a confidence thing being signed, it's not the be-all and end-all.'

The Blizzards' début album, *A Public Display of Affection,* was produced by Michael Beinhorn in LA and released in 2006. The singles, 'Miss Fantasia Preaches', 'Trouble' and 'Fantasy', received huge daytime radio play, making the Blizzards a household name in a very short period of time. They didn't coast on their radio success, however: they worked really hard to be a live band they could be proud of.

'The thing about Ireland is that the standard of live band is so far superior to any other place I've been. I remember the first time we played with Republic of Loose and I looked at the band driving home that night I said, 'That's the level we need to get to live," (because we were all over the place) and Moff, our manager, turned around and said, "Well the last thing you're going to do is go into a rehearsal room five days a week to get like that. You're playing shitholes for the next

three weeks until you're good live; you can only become good live by playing in front of people."

'We were never obsessed with getting out of Ireland,' explains Bresy. 'We never rushed. If we had gone to the UK two years ago on hands and knees we would have failed. Now I'm a more confident songwriter and a more confident front man, and we're a more confidant live band, and we have the egotistical thing now that every band needs. We know that if you put us in a showcase in London with four bands we will blow them all off the stage, and that's the confidence you need.'

Domino Effect followed in 2008 with further hit singles 'Trust Me I'm A Doctor' and 'The Reason'. The third single from *Domino Effect*, 'Postcards', showed a more sensitive, mature side to the band and their songwriting ability. It is a heartfelt, emotional ballad and it too became a massive radio hit.

'When we first wrote that song, it was the first time I thought; that's as honest as I'm ever going to get on a track. It's a very touching song but the original cut of it was almost too emotional. If we had released it as a single a lot of people would have known who it was about and we didn't want that, so we had to rewrite it. That song was written in forty minutes: the best songs just come like that. When we wrote it I remember giving it to the person who was affected by it and I said, this is just for you, for no one else. We didn't write it for an album, or for a single; we didn't write it to get on the radio: we wrote it to comfort this person. We sent them the CD and the first thing they sent back was, "You have to release this, for us you have to release it," so that's what we did.'

Bresy is signed to Universal Publishing in the UK. He is a prolific songwriter and knows that some of the songs he comes up with won't suit the Blizzards or their live shows: 'I can write what I want because I *love* indie music, I *love* left-of-centre music and I *love* pop music. I think there's no music in the world I don't like. I have a portfolio of hundreds of tracks that will just never work with us.'

'I didn't sign to Universal Publishing, I signed to the publisher I really liked, a guy called Dougy Bruce. He had a huge repertoire of brilliant pop acts, like Lily Allen – right down my alley. Dougy actually left Universal Publishing a couple of months later and I got an even better publisher called Caroline Ellory, who signed Coldplay when they didn't even have a record deal. I've never had A&R guidance, ever, I've been basically blindfolded through this whole process. The only guidance was from Beinhorn and at that stage a producer really shouldn't have to be guiding you. A producer shouldn't be telling you what songs you're good at writing – that should be A&R. So that's what the publishing deal meant to me. I didn't care about money, I just wanted that advice and guidance and also this portfolio of music. I wanted to go, "Do you have any homes for this?"'

'I just want to become a better songwriter: that's the only thing that makes me buzz. I won't be happy until I write a flawless pop record. I listen to ELO and bands like that and I think, "This is flawless." That's what I want. The reason I know I can get there is that I take advice. I don't think I'm anywhere near the finish line because I know I'm not. I think this is the secret – not being a pig-headed musician.'

Niall started out in sport. He went to UCD on a sport scholarship for rugby, then he played for Leinster before leaving to pursue music and the band

'My love is not rugby, it never was, it just happened that I was 6'6",' laughs Niall. 'And I could run, so I kind of landed in a rugby career. I came up to UCD where rugby had incredible status in that area of Dublin and I realised I could beat up posh Dublin people and get away with it!' he jokes. 'Towards the later years when I got a professional contract, I was going, "This is not what I want, it's too intense." I was watching people coming out the other end of their careers not being able to walk and I thought, "I'm not doing this; sacrificing my body for something I'm not really keen on." Playing and playing professionally are two different ball games and that's why I have more respect for the Irish rugby team than anybody in the world. Some of them are mates of mine and I know what they go through: it's really intense.'

Niall had been jamming with the lads (who would become the Blizzards) at weekends in Mullingar, all guys he knew from school. 'The lads said, "OK, Bresy, you need a weekend off, come down," because they knew rugby wasn't enjoyable for me and I was getting injured all the time. My only outlet was to go down to Mullingar every weekend, go to Dec's bedroom and play music.'

Apparently it was not a given that Bresy would be the singer of the Blizzards: 'Lynchy is a great singer and he wrote songs. He is a big folk fan and he has always been an amazing folk songwriter but he said, "I don't really like playing it, though," and I said, "I have a few songs…"'

'Most of the time Lynchy and I sing together anyway and Justin can sing too. Out of the three of us I would have the more commanding voice but because I don't have a really great voice, I need to use the two guys beside me to really back it up and do the harmonies, which is kind of what we're known for.'

'We recorded an EP then and at that stage I rang my agent, a South African guy who just happened to share an office with Marcus Russell, the Oasis manager. I said, "James, I'm retiring from rugby. I'm really sorry: it's just not in me any more." He was a bit upset because I was his first Irish signing and because at this stage I had played for the Irish Under-21s. He said, "Why are you doing this? Are you sure you're making the right choice?" I said, "Well, you're going to laugh at me but I want to pursue music." And instead of going, "You fucking twat," he goes, "Have you any EPs?" "I do actually, why?" "Because I sit beside Marcus Russell."'

'I sent the EP over on the Wednesday. On Friday we were playing our second-ever gig in Eamonn Dorans and Marcus Russell flew over for it. He goes, "I love your EP, I love it." We were like, "Jesus Christ!" We were only starting and he saw that because we were all over the place live but he goes, "I love your EP," and he flew over and back a few times. Then I got the guts to go, "Well, if Marcus Russell thinks we've got something going on then I can give up, so I rang my parents and said, "Da, I'm finished." He was amazing because it did break his heart. My mum's a music teacher and she had stomach ulcers worrying about me playing rugby. I was the kind of stupid gimp who would always put his head where it shouldn't be. I'd come home and mum would be, "Oh God!"

Dad's point was, "Why are you doing music. You have a degree – would you not go and work?" So I went working in a bank: I lasted six months. My da said, "Ah, you can't give up on this as well!" I said, "Dad, you *have* to let me do music."'

The problem was that Niall's brother is a successful musician (he now works as a producer in Glasgow) and he and his band had signed a massive deal with Sony. They recorded an album with Harry Connick Junior in New Orleans and then got dropped by fax. It's your typical, heartbreaking, nightmare label story. 'So Dad was always sceptical,' explains Bresy. 'He was like, "Niall, there are thousands of bands in Ireland, what will make you stand out?" I said, "I really don't know, Dad."'

Bresy was able to learn from his brother's negative experience and received excellent advice from him early on: 'He warned me. He was the first person to say, "Do not sign a UK deal, sign a priority act deal. Don't look at money, don't worry about money, don't ask for a big advance." He's done everything and he's been in a band and he's seen the dark side of the labels.'

Like many successful bands, the Blizzards have a little extra something on their side: a good manager. 'I knew Moff [Justin Moffatt] from playing music in Mullingar. He used to play a lot, he's a musician. He said he was looking for someone he could be really passionate about and put everything into, and he wanted only one act. We gave him the EP and he came up to see us and said, "I would love to manage ye." He's not made one wrong decision yet, which is strange for a manager,' laughs Bresy. 'Not one! And he seems to get on incredibly well with the label. It was the best decision we ever made.'

The Blizzards may be signed to a major label but they don't sit back and wait for things to happen, Bresy and Moff spend a lot of time at the label. 'We know that the ball is as much in our court as it is theirs. We're not stupid and they know we're not stupid. We know for every album the Killers sell, if we sell one it's worth five to Universal Ireland because we're *their* act. They can't come in and say, "Well, the Killers have sold 10,000." We say, "Well, we sold 10,000, which is worth 50,000." They know they're not playing with fools, so they don't treat us like fools. It's business and I like getting involved with it. The band means everything to me so I'm not going to let somebody it obviously doesn't mean that much to make big decisions without my knowing about it.'

'People respect Moff because he doesn't lie and he never bullshits. He's honest and the good guy always wins. It's a small industry here and if you fuck around with the wrong people, if you piss off one venue, they hate you for life. So we try not to piss anybody off! That's the key, I think.'

As a Mullingar man, Bresy is aware that there are plenty of bands in the country with chips on their shoulders, complaining that they don't have a chance because, 'It's all up in Dublin.' 'It's not all up in Dublin. The best bands I've seen in Ireland, none of them have been from Dublin, that's the truth. You have to accept that Dublin is the capital city of the country and everything is going to gravitate towards it: that's where the rehearsal rooms are, the studios. I think it's bollocks and we've never used it as an excuse: It's work ethic and songs.

'Music isn't centralised in Ireland and that's the good thing about it, Fred are one of my favourite bands, the Kanyu Tree in Galway, Giveamanakick – these are the bands, that I would pay to watch. If you want to use that as an excuse maybe you shouldn't get into the music industry because if that's an excuse what other ones are there? The radio aren't playing you because the radio are pricks? The radio has a job to do and that's the one thing we've always accepted.'

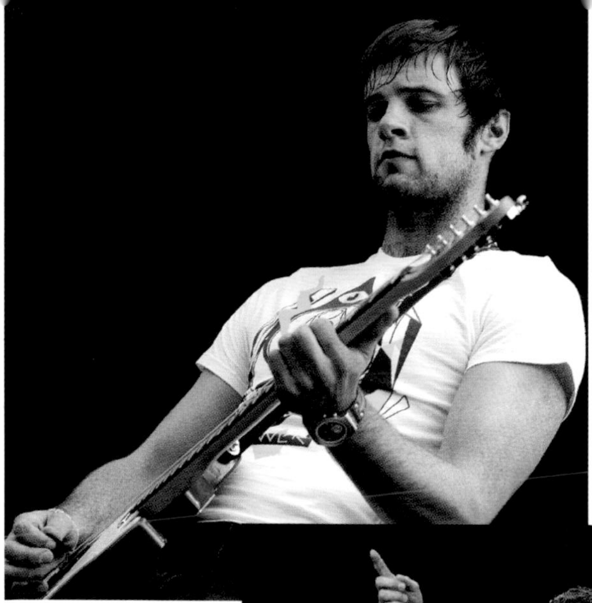

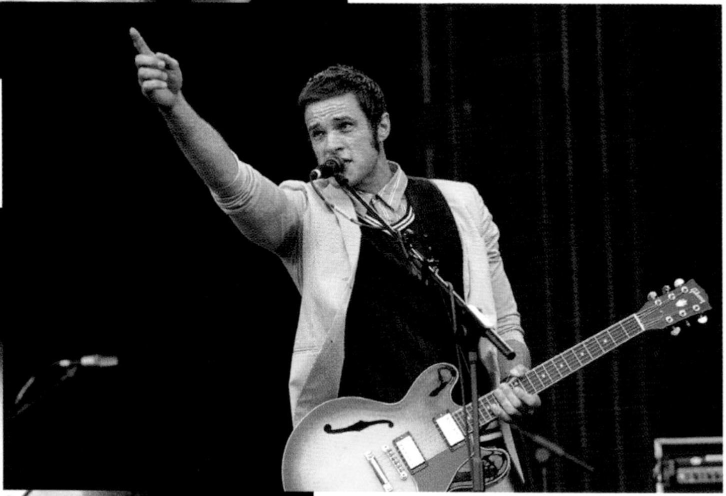

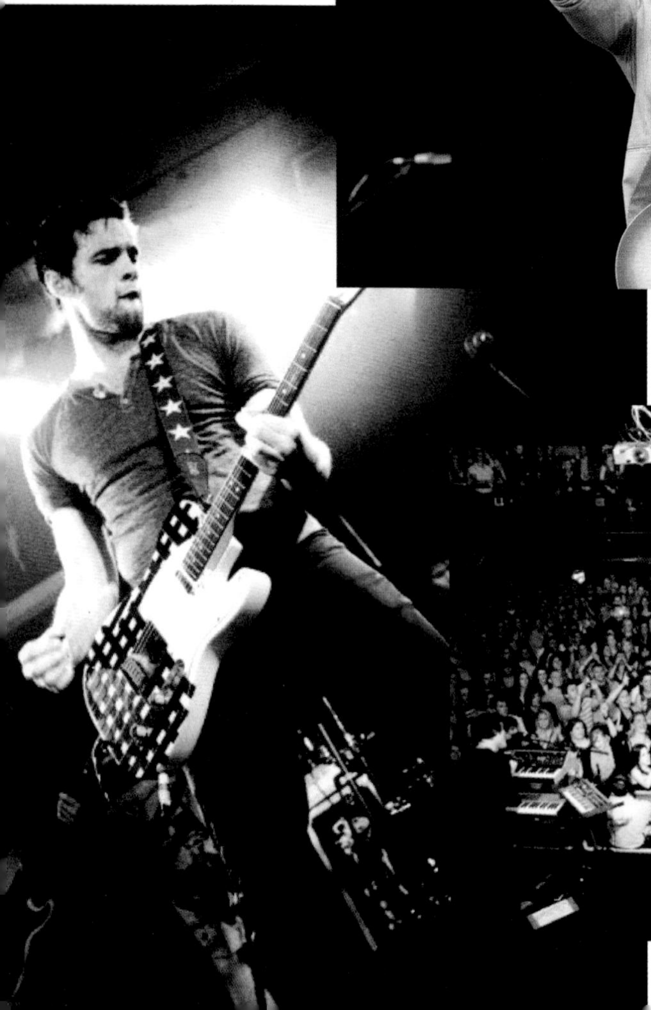

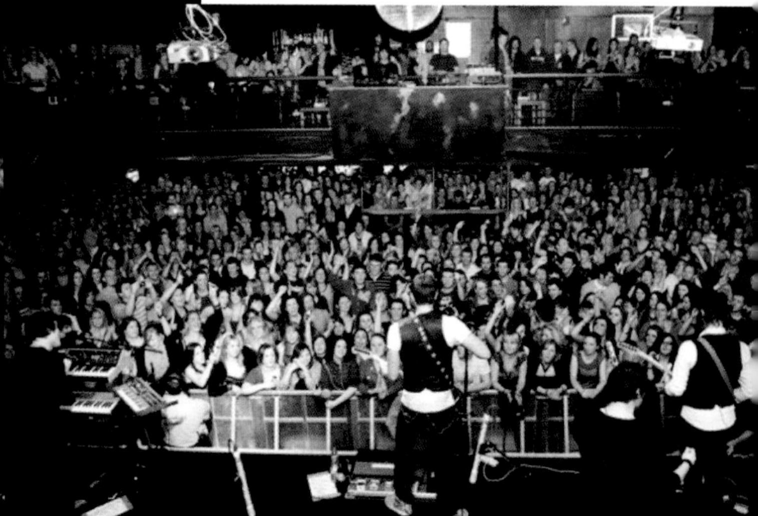

© JUSTIN MOFFATT

The Blizzards don't cry that they are not played by alternative radio. They know they are a band better suited to pop radio and they are delighted by the huge daytime radio support they have received. Size of venue does not seem to be an important factor to the Blizzards either: they are not writing with stadiums in mind. But they *are* ambitious.

'I certainly don't want to play a stadium as a support act in front of the janitor and the security men. That's of no interest to us; that's demoralising for a band. Just to say you supported such a big artist? I would rather play in a crowded 200-capacity shithole: people sweating two feet away from you. I'd like it to be organic.'

Like many Irish bands at the top of their game at home, the Blizzards are concentrating on other territories. They followed early advice, took their time, worked on their craft and waited until they felt they were ready to really go for it in the UK: 'The one thing we've always wanted for the Blizzards is progression. If we all thought we had to tour Ireland four, five times a year for the next ten years I don't think we'd do it because that's not progression for us. That's not us turning our back on the Irish scene; we've done what we can do here.'

'My motivation is essentially this,' says Bresy. 'In an ideal world for every album the Blizzards get to record, we recoup and get to make another. We have a five-album deal in the UK and I just want to get better and better and better. Hopefully with a fourth, fifth album I will be in a position where I am incredibly happy with my songwriting ability, my production ability, I'm incredibly happy to be in this band. Essentially, I want to bring this band as far as they want to go and as far as I'm able to go as a songwriter.'

The Coronas

Band Members

Danny O'Reilly
Graham Knox
Conor Egan
Dave McPhillips

Albums
Heroes or Ghosts
Tony Was an Ex-Con

EPs
Corona – Live at the Voodoo Lounge
Corona

Label
3ú Records

Manager
Jim Lawless

Websites
http://thecoronas.net
www.MySpace.com/coronaband

*DANNY O'REILLY REPRESENTED THE
BAND FOR THE INTERVIEW.*

The Coronas' success is due in no small part to the energy they have together on stage. The fact that lead singer Danny O'Reilly is usually grinning from ear to ear probably helps too. He has an affable, open, friendly nature that makes him virtually impossible not to like – and he writes very catchy songs. The Coronas' début album, *Heroes Or Ghosts*, was packed full of infectious anthems, songs of summers away and partying all night – songs that make you want to sing along and punch at the air during the chorus. It's no surprise that they captured the hearts of students across the country. But they didn't just win over the students – they won over daytime radio too, achieving platinum sales in the process.

Releases of *Heroes Or Ghosts* in Japan and the UK followed before the band headed back to studio to record their second album, *Tony Was an Ex-Con*.

So how did a young band on a small domestic indie label achieve this without a massive advertising campaign or marketing spend?

The Coronas didn't quite reverse the traditional format of: record album, retain PR company, release single to media, play gigs, release album, release second single, tour – but they certainly shook it up. The band had sold out Whelans before they had even been written about in the press. Suddenly, there were questions flying around media circles asking who the Coronas were. Were they a boy band? Were they one of those *You're A Star* contestants?

When the press eventually caught up with the lads, they realised that they were not a manufactured boy band but friends from school who had been gigging away quietly for years, building up a substantial following in the process. They also realised that Danny's mother was the famous Irish singer, Mary Black. Inevitable interest in that fact soon followed, an interest that Danny finds somewhat bemusing, because to him, she's just a normal mother.

'It's funny that people think: so what sort of effect did it have? The whole Mary Black thing. But she was just the same as the other mothers, just supportive – and she never forced it [music] upon us. My other brother works nine-to-five now and doesn't really play music and my sister is in college. It was never like, "Well, this is the family way…" Never! It was just the way it happened.'

Danny's parents may be steeped in folk and traditional music but they had very open minds when it came to the music he was into.

'When we were growing up, I would put on a Radiohead album and my Mum would be like, "That's amazing!" She would love it and she would never, ever tell me what to listen to. But then she would say, "Have a listen to this album." I remember when I was really young and my Mum and Dad gave me *Revolver* [The Beatles, 1966] because I had been listening to Oasis and I was like, "What the hell. This is great!" I always remember my Mum kept saying, "You have to get this album, *Rumours* [Fleetwood Mac, 1977]. I bought it for Christmas and I was like, "This is the best record I have ever heard." So it's great to have that but they never ever forced it on us.'

It turns out that Danny is not alone in the band to have had a musical upbringing. Graham 'Knoxy' Knox had a pretty cool musical upbringing too. His father owns a record store and used to be a DJ.

'He used to DJ in Old Wesley and other places around Dublin in the late 1970s. Knoxy probably has a much wider range of musical taste than I do because he has been surrounded by CDs his whole life, whereas I have been surrounded by Mary Black CDs…which is great as well!'

Danny and Knoxy went to school together but their friendship goes even further back than that: the two were born within two weeks of each other and they have been friends since they were babies.

By their early teens, Danny's older brother and cousins were in bands and the boys thought they were amazing and wanted to give it a try themselves. By fifteen, they were in their first proper band. They went to Newtownmountkennedy to record with Gavin Ralston (former Picturehouse band member) and there they recorded their first three-track demo.

'We were listening to it the other week for a laugh,' grins Danny. 'Some of those tunes aren't that bad, actually! We could come back to it for a dodgy third album if we are missing a few songs!'

Their first gig was in an afternoon all-ages show in the Clifton Court Hotel, just off O'Connell Bridge in Dublin, when they were around sixteen. They had about fifteen friends there to watch them and they played a few covers and did one of their own songs, Danny recalls: 'We always found gigs, even when we were under-age, at least one every two or three months.'

At that time, they were called Kiros, with Conor Doyle as lead singer, Danny on backing vocals and guitar, Knoxy on bass and Egan on drums. Even at that early age, tensions were developing and causing problems, a fact that amuses Danny greatly on reflection: 'It just wasn't working out for us and we weren't really getting on, so we sort of went our separate ways. Then myself, Egan and Knoxy started getting together again and jamming just because we missed it. So we were a three-piece for four or five years. We were just called Corona then.'

Corona started gigging around and developing a bit of a following. They recorded a gig supporting Pugwash in Voodoo called *Live At The Voodoo Lounge EP*, followed by *The Corona* EP in early 2005. Initially, they were selling this for €5 at gigs, which proved successful enough. Then they started handing out the EP to anyone interested, allowing people to copy it for free. Then they went on holidays.

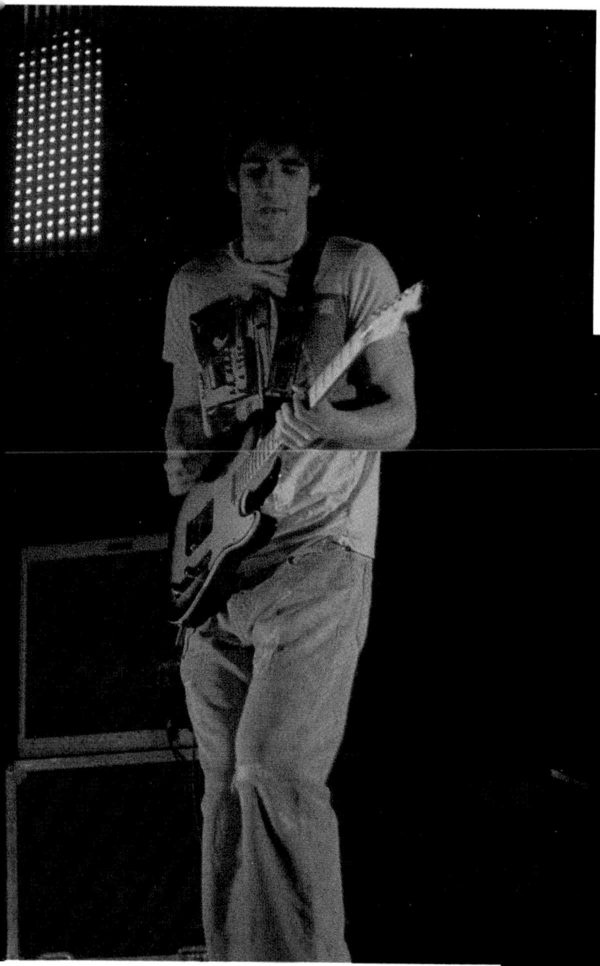
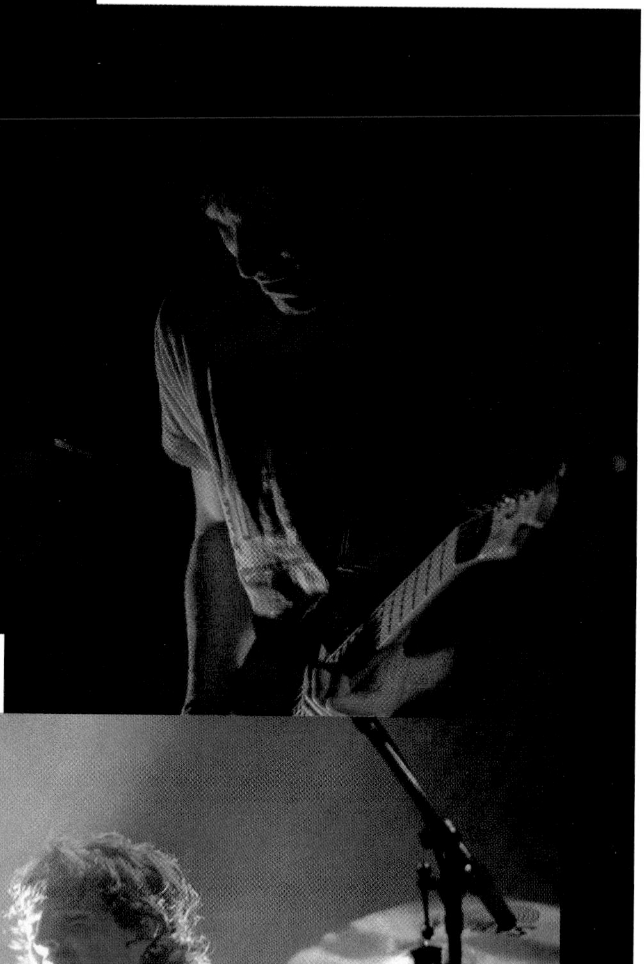
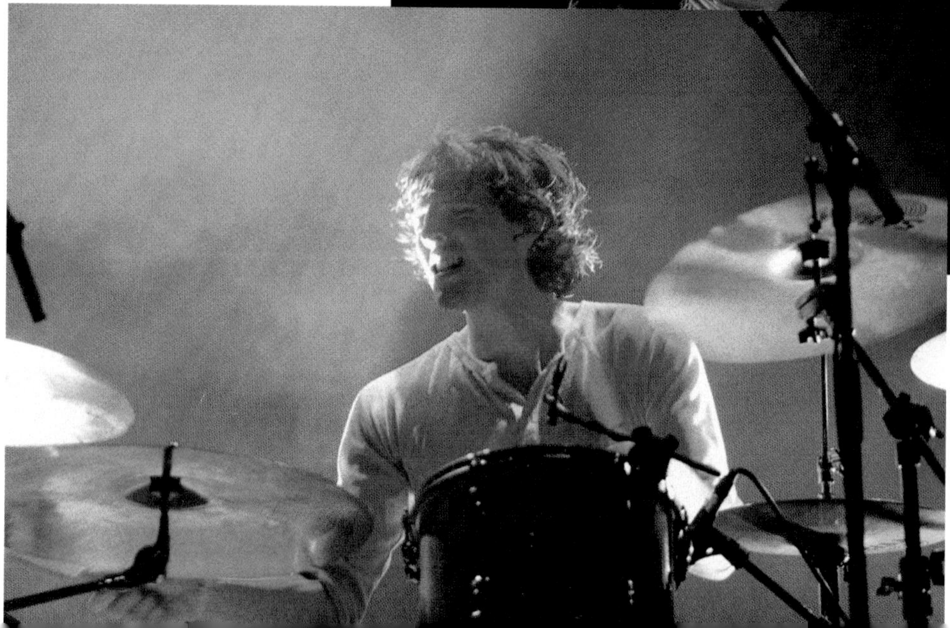

© DARA MUNNIS

Danny and Knoxy went to Vancouver after their second year in college, when they were about nineteen. They were staying in a fraternity house at the University of British Columbia, or UBC as it's known, when they bumped into a guy who was playing guitar in a circle at a party. Rather than being a new Canadian acquaintance as expected, he turned out to be a fellow Irishman: Dave McPhillips from Monkstown. They had some friends in common back home so they hit it off right away and ended up playing together virtually every night in the circle of music that existed in the house.

When they came back to Dublin, Danny had a master plan to bring Dave into the band, but Egan had not been in Vancouver (and had not even met Dave) and with Danny, Knoxy and Egan having been best friends since childhood, it was going to be a difficult sell. They had a gig on that week so Danny suggested getting Dave in to do one song for the laugh: 'We were doing a gig at Slatterys and he came up and we did "The Wait" by the Band and he sang and we did the harmonies and stuff and the lads loved it.' McPhillips was in.

'I think deep down I always knew that we were going to need a change in line-up because I am just not a good enough guitarist to make a three-piece,' Danny admits. 'I think if you are going to be a three-piece band, you have to have an amazing guitarist who just knows about pedals and electric guitar playing, and you know, can do *everything*, because I really can't.'

The new four-piece decamped to a cottage in Wicklow: 'We locked ourselves in for two and a half weeks and didn't shower and played music non-stop. It was just amazing – it worked from the start. We were so lucky, because if it hadn't worked, I think we would have just filtered out.'

'Dave always says he joined when all the hard gigs had been done and we already had a bit of a following. He thinks he joined when the party was in full flow, whereas I think he sort of saved a sinking ship.'

The Coronas continued their studies while they grew their fan base, supporting everyone they got a chance to and playing every college ball offered: 'We stuck it out and finished our degrees, which was a good thing to do and made our parents happy. Poor Dave had to do his thesis while we were recording the album. He was literally researching in the studio on the laptop, trying to get it done.'

They were still in college when they first sold out Whelans. The band thought there was something going on in the Village because there were so many people out on the street: 'It was so surprising for us because we were just coming from lectures. I remember Jim ringing me and saying, "It's fucking packed, lads!!" There were touts outside selling tickets. We were just like, "What the fuck?" That had never happened before.'

Danny is very humble about the accomplishment, figuring that when people went away for the summer, they took the *Corona* EP with them and when they got bored of their own CDs, they gave it a listen. The band came back after the summer to find people singing the words to all the songs at the gig.

'I think it would be so hard to get someone to listen to a new album like that now because they go away with their iPod and listen to whatever is on that, so I think we were just lucky,' Danny muses. 'The gigs had been going *relatively* well, but we just presumed that in order to sell out Whelans, you had to be a big band that had a load of hype about you and you were in *Hot Press* and people were talking about you and stuff: we never had any of that! No one mentioned us in the press for another year after that: a month after the album was released was the first time.'

Once their début album was recorded, the lads thought that they should do a few gigs to get the single going. An old teacher had been in touch with them and asked them to come back to the school to play a twice annual lunchtime gig for all the student bands in Terenure College, which they did, charging €5 at the door and donating it all to charity.

They ended up doing six or seven gigs in different schools all around Dublin, which proved a massive help to the band. Not only were they playing to incredibly receptive audiences, giving them an instant fan base, they were having fun.

The album went to Number 24 in the charts, but then dropped off the radar completely until Dublin's FM104 started playing 'San Diego Song', after the band had performed an acoustic cover on the *Strawberry Alarm Clock* breakfast show.

'We did Justin Timberlake's "My Love" and they got a massive text response from all our fans,' Danny recalls. 'They said, "This is the biggest text response for a band that we have ever had."'

When 'San Diego Song' went to Number 1 in their airplay charts, other stations followed suit and started playing it: 'I think people thought we were a pop band or *You're A Star* band or something. We didn't do anything about it, because we didn't really know how to – we were just happy that people were listening to us.'

TV appearances soon followed, including *The Café*, *The Late Late Show* and *Other Voices*, but getting national radio play was a much bigger deal for them: 'I remember Dan Hegarty playing our first two singles late at night on 2fm and thinking that was great, but daytime radio play was just huge for us.'

The Coronas had huge support from national radio with DJs like Ray Foley and Rick O'Shea really getting behind them. Daytime radio play is notoriously hard to get and Danny thinks they were very lucky, that other Irish bands had helped make it possible: 'I think we came along at the right time and rode the crest of the waves that the Blizzards and the Loose [Republic of Loose] laid for us.'

Danny is such a natural front man that it's hard to believe that he was not always the singer, that he ever suffered from nerves or got stressed out on stage.

'It's funny, I was the second man in our first band, I was just backing vocals and hiding behind my guitar and trying to do a few harmonies here and there and after a while I was like, "I want to get out there and sing!"'

'I remember one piece of advice that my mum gave me, which I always thought was good and always helped us: even if it's crap on stage and sounds awful on stage and you're not really enjoying the gig, just look like you are enjoying it because it rubs off on the crowd. I always remember that and I always *do* enjoy it, even if it is going badly, because at the end of the day, you have to remember it's the thing that you want to do with your life and we're really lucky to be able to do it. So it's not false but she did say, "Just always make sure that they *know* you're enjoying it," and I do. I just buzz off the crowd.'

Good advice and radio play are not the only things the band have had on their side. Jim Lawless has been managing the band pretty much since they left school. Jim was a year ahead of them in school and as school captain was always organising things, so the lads asked him to give them a hand. He said yes and what began as helping out mushroomed, as the relationship and band developed over the years.

'He is a big part of the band. It's like he is a member. Every gig is split five ways and if it was right, he should probably get more for the work he does and the lack of credit he gets. He is sort of like our manager and our record company: he does everything. I can't speak highly enough of him: without him, I think we would really be fucked – we'd still be jamming in a garage saying we are going to record our EP soon!'

The affection all the Coronas have for each other is apparent when Danny speaks about his band mates: 'You hear about other bands having serious fights and tantrums, throwing people off buses and throwing people off tour and we always hear these stories and say, "Can you imagine that happening to us?!" because we are just never like that at all! We do have our time apart, but we are just so used to one another as well. When we get home from tour, Knoxy will just ring me up and say, "Will we go for pints?"

The reality is that it can be hard to mix band life with 'normal' life, as musicians tend to hold similar hours to vampires. This causes difficulties when your friends from college are now

IN BLOOM - THE CORONAS

holding day jobs: 'We will get home from a tour on a Tuesday night thinking, "End of tour party!" so you're ringing a friend up at 9:30 and they are like, "I'm in bed – I've got work tomorrow."'

There have been major labels sniffing about since the success of the Coronas' début album, *Heroes and Ghosts*, but they are content with the support they have from independent label, 3u. While they are open to major label deals for other territories (they are signed to JVC in Japan) they don't wait around for offers to keep moving forward.

In keeping with that independent spirit, they self-funded a tour of the US in 2008 with money they had earned gigging. They played a wide range of small venues, from Irish bars to frat houses from one coast to the other. Not only was it a great trip, it was a productive one. Their agent in the UK has a sister company in the States and sent important people along to see them, introducing them to influential contacts they hope to work with in the future.

Their Japanese deal with JVC came about in a very unusual fashion, when a Japanese PR agent saw them while she was in Ireland with Paul Brady. Dara Munnis, a good friend of the Coronas, met her at a Paul Brady gig, where his father was the sound man, and invited her to see the Coronas play. She went and she liked them so much that she returned to Japan with a stack of Coronas albums under her arm and a promise to get them a record deal. To their great surprise, email contact was soon being made by various labels, with JVC winning the battle for their signature. A subsequent promo trip to Japan went so well that they hope to repeat it every year.

'We are on the same label as the Prodigy and Feeder,' enthuses Danny. 'They just treated us so well: cars from the airport, everything organised, it was like *Spinal Tap*!'

And so to album number two. Having been very happy with the work of Dublin musician and producer Joe Chester on their début, it was very tempting to go the same route for the second album, but they felt that it might be playing it too safe, that they should take a risk and try someone new. They started listening to albums they loved and compiled a list of producers. One of them was John Cornfield, the UK legend whose previous credits include Muse, Razorlight, Oasis and Supergrass, and a man who knows how to capture energy on an album, something the lads were really keen to achieve. Cornfield loved the tunes, so the album was recorded at the Sawmills Studio in Cornwall, England.

Tony Was an Ex-Con was released in Ireland on 3ú Records on 25 September 2009. It was preceded by a national tour as special guests to the Script and the release of lead single 'Listen Dear'. Sold-out gigs and fan frenzy continues for the Coronas as talks with major labels about licensing and further releases are underway.

'We have massive ambitions to play everywhere and to try and get our album out in as many places as we can,' says Danny. We don't put ourselves under too much pressure but we are very excited about the songs we have. I'm really hoping that it will take off and that we will be able to go for it and you know, take over the world... big time!'

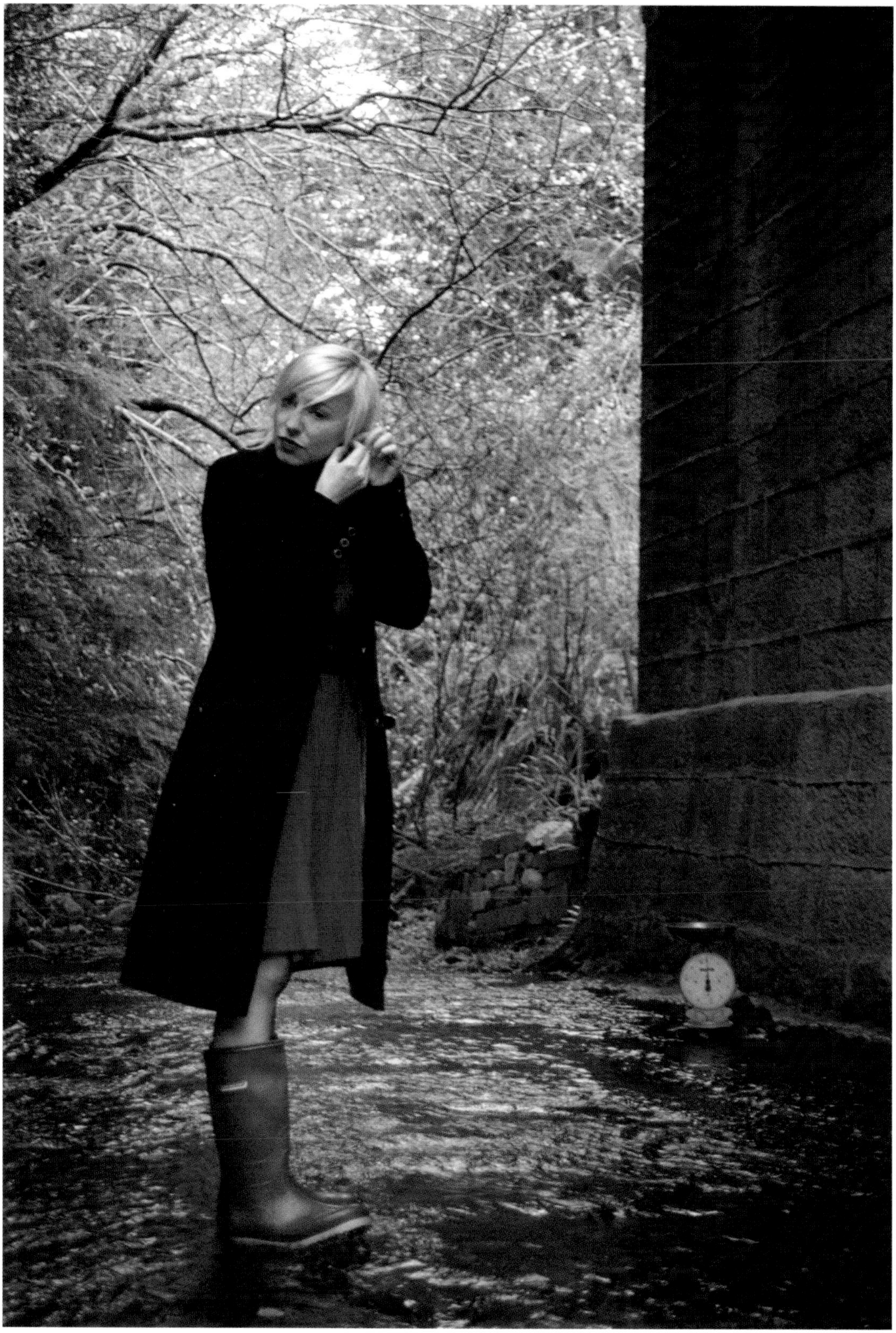

Cathy Davey

Artist
Cathy Davey

Albums
Something Ilk
Tales of Silversleeve
The Nameless

Label
Hammer Toe Records

Manager
Oliver Walsh

Websites
www.cathydavey.ie
www.MySpace.com/cathydavey

Cathy Davey has the sort of sweet shyness and easy humour that disarm you instantly. Her new-found independence seems really to suit her and to have further stimulated an already enviable talent. Cathy's creativity, individuality and voice have already left a huge imprint on the Irish musical landscape.

Her journey to independence and to the critical and popular success she enjoys today has not been an easy one – at least not in the beginning. Cathy is really honest about how difficult the recording of her first album, *Something Ilk*, was for her, and talks openly about the stresses of a major label deal when you're not yet ready: 'I just didn't have it, I didn't have the experience, I didn't have the right mind frame for it and I didn't have *it*.'

She laughs about it all, now that it's a distant memory, and cracks self-deprecating jokes about her early extreme shyness.

Cathy is a singer, a songwriter and a multi-instrumentalist: she self-produced her last two albums. She has recorded three albums, the first two with major label backing and the latest independently. Her second album, *Tales Of Silversleeve,* was shortlisted for the 2007 Choice Music Prize Album of the Year and received extensive radio support nationally. She has toured the UK, Europe and Ireland numerous times including a sold-out Olympia Theatre show, various TV appearances and a Meteor Award for Best Female Artist.

Her gigs have a reputation for warmth, harmony and excellent musicianship.

Cathy comes from a creative family but didn't have a musical upbringing in the traditional sense: 'I had a good family nest for doing something that involved spending time on your own and messing on your own and finding out what you're good at.'

'My mum is an artist and poet and my dad is a musician but they were in their own areas of work, and then they would come out and not bring what they were working on into the family. So it was just a house, a very quiet house, of people in their own heads and that was really, really natural. So I was always prone to and destined and doomed to do the same!'

Cathy got into art and music when she was very young. She first started playing the piano after her sister went to lessons: it came naturally.

'My sister was very studious and smart and she could sight-read, and I couldn't sight-read, so I would just listen to what she was playing and copy it on piano and then change the bits that I didn't like and that sort of started me writing.'

'Dad is a musician and he writes music and we understood that music was something that you wrote and you didn't listen to, because nobody listened to music in the house. My Mum had one Leonard Cohen album that she would listen to when she could bear it but music wasn't something that you would spend your time listening to: it wasn't a form or relaxation. I never thought of it as something I was enjoying, it was just something that was done.'

When one doesn't come from a musical background, it's easy to romanticise what growing up in a musical family would be like. You picture a *Sound Of Music*-type scenario of children and parents singing around the kitchen table at family gatherings. But it wasn't really like that. Cathy and her sister saw their father perform throughout their childhood but they didn't really hear him in the house: 'He was in the basement or somewhere in the garage with the piano – we weren't allowed go down!' giggles Cathy.

'Other people who have come from musical backgrounds, there is a joy about music and playing music and knowing the names of styles of music that they like. We were never ever like that. It wasn't like a pastime or your favourite programme or anything that you would understand in those terms. It wasn't a joyful musical family sharing their passions.'

Cathy didn't have any formal music lessons: she picked up instruments herself. 'I remember I did a music class in school but it was gobbledegook,' she recalls. 'But I am dyslexic and

I didn't find that out till afterwards, so I'd say that's probably why none of the dots made sense or the logic behind it: someone trying to articulate a harmony to you, I just didn't understand why you would have to put it into words!' Cathy laughs and says, 'I think I actually thought that they were beneath me because they had to understand it in mathematical terms and not intuition, and I didn't want to be part of it because it just freaked me out!'

Things moved on from piano when Cathy hit her teens: 'I got into Guns 'N' Roses because the boy I liked was into Guns 'N' Roses. I got an electric guitar for my birthday but it didn't make any sense to me, so I traded it in for an acoustic guitar.'

She thinks the start of her songs was her childhood poetry: 'I would be writing little pieces of music and singing gobbledegook but then I was writing a lot of poetry and finally when I was about seventeen, I started putting it all together and reckoning that I could make songs out of them.'

Her love of music was encouraged while she was studying art in Thomastown in Kilkenny. 'I had some really lovely friends who gave me two grand when I was about nineteen or twenty because they heard me sing songs and they wanted me to do more with it. So I bought my first electric piano and a nice guitar with that and started recording my demos on a four-track.'

It wasn't until she finished college when Cathy was twenty-two that she started to perform in front of people. Her boyfriend at the time was in a Dublin band called Bionic and they would play Eamon Dorans. He was an artist and wanted to take a break for a while so the band learned her songs and they did a few gigs. 'It was pretty horrible because I had never played in front of anyone before,' Cathy recalls. 'Then I did one gig in the Ha'penny Bridge Inn where my current manager [Oliver Walsh] came to see me and it was like, "OK, you don't have to do any more of

that," because it was horrific! It was the most terrifying thing.'

Cathy had written the lyrics for a couple of songs and sung on Ken McHugh's Autamata album, *My Sanctuary* [2002]. An A&R man from EMI Ireland had heard 'Jellyman', one of the singles Cathy featured on, and asked her to do a few demos for them. She recorded them with Ken.

Between her home demos and the one she had recorded with Ken, Cathy had enough material to record an album. Oliver had heard all her demos and asked Cathy if she wanted to try and get a deal? She said, "Sure," and Oliver went to England.

Looking back, Cathy thinks that people made a lot of assumptions about her. 'I think everyone was convinced that I was bound to be fabulous at playing live and that I was bound to be into dresses and designer things, so I think they made up their mind that I was going to be something that they wanted me to be. Which is more fool them really, because I was incredibly shy and I was really, really against designer fashion and stylists and anything that involved trying to look like aesthetics are more important than music. That sounds very pompous but it was so important because it had never entered my head that that should be a part of it.'

Cathy was signed, more or less on the spot, to Parlophone Records. Major label deals can be pretty daunting when you are young and new to it all. It can be particularly hard to speak up when you are unsure – because maybe these people know best?

'You have no idea if you are being unreasonable,' she admits. 'I was always aware that you should say yes to things, to get an educated idea of what you are saying no to in the future but I always *knew*. So when I tried to say no, no one was there with me to say, "if you don't want to do it, that's fine."'

No one was ever nasty to her: 'It was always, "You're being a little unreasonable. That scarf looks fabulous on you!" 'It would always come to the crunch when just the tiniest thing would tip it and I would be like, "What the fuck am I doing?" ' laughs Cathy.

'It's funny, I can't say I regret it because it has brought me here to my third album and I am happy now doing it on my own (they dropped me last year) but it was a pretty stressful thing to be signed to people who presume that you will come round when they push money in your face.'

Cathy thinks it would have helped if she had played in front of friends when she was young: 'I think that's the flaw with developing what you do on your own without some kind of core family that you call a band around you.'

'I had no interaction with an outside world of music or how people reacted or what they aspired to. So when I got into it, I realised that most people who were doing music and who really rose to the occasion in studios had always wanted to be there and when they got there, it was *their time* and they were able to perform because they had been working towards that. I just hadn't thought it through. I had no idea I would feel so [uncomfortable].'

Being signed to a major label came with the opportunity to work with famous producers in expensive studios: 'I worked with Ken Nelson, who is Coldplay's producer, and I did a week with him and it was all sort of big: big time, top dollar.'

'He stood me in the middle of the studio when it was time to do vocals, after the backing track was done, and after they said, "We have done fifty-six takes and it's not getting any better." It was like – I can't sing in tune, in here, in this world! I can't do it in front of you!' Cathy laughs. 'So we scrapped that and tried a different route but that's how the first album was made. I did it

with Ben Hillier [Blur, Elbow, Depeche Mode] in the end but the same problem arose. I couldn't play in front of him or sing in front of him.'

Cathy explains: 'The more time that goes by, the more money is being wasted and the more laboured each take is becoming, the worse it gets. I just didn't have it, I didn't have the experience, I didn't have the right mind frame for it and I didn't have *it*. I didn't have presence of voice, I could hear it when it was coming back, it sounded to me like someone who had not got a thing that's special.'

It's obvious that Cathy has reflected on that time a great deal: 'I used to think it was lack of ego but I think maybe it's massive ego that would make me so über aware of people listening to it and listening to what you commit to tape. That it's too much, the power of what you are making is too much – so much that I couldn't live up to it. Whatever it is in your body that makes you want to run instead of singing out and saying, "This is the best!" Cathy giggles. 'I don't know what the hell it was but it was a fucking disaster!'

With such a stressful first experience of recording, it would be understandable if it took the joy out of music for Cathy or turned her off the industry entirely but it didn't make her question her love of music, just the method by which it was recorded: 'I always knew the method for me was at home, without anyone, but I though the more that I did it in front of other people, the easier it would get, and that's true to a certain extent.'

'Now that I am independent, I actually feel that I have flourished. I'm so happy playing now and I am so happy with what I am writing that I am able to play it really well live.'

There is a story that has circulated about Cathy, a myth that developed after her first album came out. The story goes that she was due to perform on Jools Holland but her appendix ruptured and she couldn't play so K.T. Tunstall was given her spot on the show as a last-minute replacement. This would be the spot that gave K.T. Tunstall her big break and made her the name she is today.

It turns out there were two separate stories blurred into one through Chinese whispers. 'The appendix burst when I was on tour with Supergrass,' Cathy reveals. 'Which would have been a really good tour for me to build up some courage. I think it was two or three days into it, so I missed three weeks and got the last two days – damn it,' she says, laughing.

As for the K.T. Tunstall part of the story, it wasn't really linked to Cathy: 'I was singing songs that I didn't really like. I didn't know how to play them or to sing to people. I didn't know how to stand on stage and I was apologetic. So the people from Jools Holland came along to see me one night and I did one of my usual shows, which was apologetic and short and maybe a quick mumble and going through the songs and it was unimpressive. I think it was just after the appendix thing, so I was probably a bit more shit than I would have been before but if I had been in flying form, I still wasn't ready for it.'

'I really wasn't anything to talk about at that stage. The only thing that was happening was that I had a whole load of good demos that were then rerecorded uncomfortably and I had a big machine behind me and was blonde and I had tits. So they could present me in a such a way but you know, I really shouldn't have been there. I shouldn't have *let* myself be there either but at the same time I had to be there to be here now, so I can't see any way around it.'

The hard part for Cathy was feeling like she was getting opportunities that she had not yet earned: 'You are getting all the privileges of someone who deserves it when you are signed and when you've got money behind you but if you've got half a brain, you know you don't deserve it.'

Cathy is resolute about it now, however: 'I feel that all the insecurities were ironed out by extreme pressure on someone who just didn't have a fucking clue! I really didn't and I knew I didn't and it's fine but those missed opportunities happened because I didn't have the goods at the time.'

'My manager, Oliver, has always believed in me an awful lot and I sometimes wonder why, because I look back and there's

IN BLOOM - CATHY DAVEY

just an uncomfortable person who's not ready to be seen in public – just a foetus!' Cathy jokes.

Cathy has not worked with a producer since her first album. She takes control of proceedings herself and brings in an engineer to record the album, or rerecord any parts of her demos she is not happy with. Liam Howe [Sneaker Pimps] came over to record *Tales Of Silversleeve*: 'He was wonderful. We hired a house in Dublin and we just put the equipment in there and he gave me such excitement for the whole thing because he *got* how to record it.'

With her third album, *The Nameless,* Cathy worked with Tommy McLaughlin, guitarist with Villagers and all-round studio wizard: 'I did about half of it with Tommy engineering and the rest on my own, a good mix, I think, of sociable recording and self-absorbed obsessing. There's a bigger batch of songs from scratch with this one, because obviously you get more confident with each album.

She feels that *Tales Of Silversleeve* was, in a sense, built around drum sounds – 'There was so much guitar music around so just to veer away from that, not in a rock sense but in a back to rhythmical sense and then try and find a melody: detouring from melody just coming from guitars' – but *The Nameless* was developed mostly on mandolin, banjo and drums.

'I had this lovely fantasy of going to France for a month with just a mandolin and writing songs that work purely on a ukelele style,' she confesses. 'Very, very simple songs that carry themselves with the most minimal accompaniment. But I brought more things and they found their way on to it and it gets boring actually, because you write a song once on one instrument and then you kind of want to challenge yourself on something else.

'I think most people, if they play one thing, they'll play pretty much anything – you don't have to be a virtuoso to make a song out of it.'

Relocating away from her Dublin home was an important part of the writing process for the new album: 'My house in Dublin had become kind of a half-way house from touring, because everyone leaves their gear there and people come to mind the dog and everyone knows when you are in so it's hard to be the loner that you need to be. So I found that I kept booking myself away for a month to write.'

Taking time away from touring and promoting was a joy for Cathy: 'It was like when I was in school or in college and I was bunking off, it was a hint of that thrill again!'

All Cathy's hard work for *Silversleeve* gave her both the desire and the financial muscle to record and release *The Nameless* independently: 'It was so exhausting and so much fun but in hindsight it was so fucking exhausting and so much time, so little time for personal life in any way and I wonder how much of being a girl who has hit thirty has to do with me going, "I want to have a personal life and I want to write music at home and I want to do film scores and I want to build my studio,"' laughs Cathy. 'But it's all nesting, in a musical way.'

'It would be lovely to be able to work at home but then, saying that, there is this little tour that I do, the Bare Bones tour and we've been sometimes playing to forty people in a tiny room and I got the biggest buzz from doing that, like nothing I have ever experienced. I remember I cried one night on stage because I was so affected by it!' she admits. 'I guess it's still about learning and reaching little pockets of people because not everyone can get to Cork, Galway, Limerick or

Belfast. But it's also about: if you are going to travel one country for a year or half a year, you may as well go see Kerry and go and see the beautiful parts.'

Thinking about the highlights of her career so far, Cathy says all it has been enjoyable since the release of *Tales Of Silversleeve*, because it had been so unenjoyable for her previously: 'Every time I would go play Cyprus Avenue, it was better that the last time: every gig was more enjoyable than the last. The Olympia was amazing because it's every Dubliner's dream to play there. It's just really romantic, walking out: you can pretend you are Edith Piaf or something. It's like it's really porous and you can use its ambience and environment to make you into a performer and I think that's what's good about it – I think it turns everyone into a performer. It's really an empowering place.'

Delorentos

Band Members

Kieran McGuinness
Ross McCormick
Ronan Yourell (Ro)
Níal Conlan

Albums

In Love with Detail
You Can Make Sound

EPs

Leave It On
Do You Realise

Label

Delorecords

Manager

Hugh Murray

Websites

www.delorentos.net
www.MySpace.com/delorentos

*KIERAN AND NÍAL REPRESENTED
DELORENTOS FOR THE INTERVIEW.*

The individual members of the band Delorentos are as likeable as they are different. Their personalities balance and bounce of each other in the most natural way: at times it's like witnessing a four-hand comedy routine. They are genuine, down to earth, funny guys with heart and a hard-working reputation.

Delorentos are a tight, melodic indie rock band with a slew of successful singles. They have a sound that moves from punchy indie rock to fragile and haunting emotional epics. Their music is hook-laden, melodic and catchy. They don't have a lead singer per se: they change singer and lead guitar by song as they see fit: Anything goes is the motto.

Their first album *In Love With Detail* was shortlisted for the Choice Music Prize in 2007 and nominated for two Meteor Awards for Best Irish band and Best Irish Album. They have crossed over into daytime radio play with many of their singles while still retaining their indie credibility and support. They have toured Ireland extensively, played every major Irish festival including high-profile supports to the Arctic Monkeys and Supergrass at Malahide Castle, and have headlined the Ambassador Theatre. They have toured Italy and the UK and performed gigs in North America. Delorentos announced that they would be breaking up after the recording of their second album *You Can Make Sound* due to the departure of Ronan Yourell (Ro) from the band. Luckily for fans the band announced that they would be staying together, a few months later, through a personal letter written by Ro.

Delorentos were formed through a combination of school friendships, members leaving and a *Buy and Sell* ad. Kieran starts at the beginning: 'I was mad into music from when I was a kid: the most mad-into-music person I knew. I'd written songs when I was ten and shown them to my dad and he'd say, "That's very good." He laughs as he remembers asking his father could he be like the Jackson 5 and other innocent but ambitious questions. Kieran continues, 'I went away for a summer and I came back and my friends had started a band. I asked if I could be in the band and they were like, "You can't play an instrument," and I was like, "Yeah, but I can sing," and they were like, "No."' Kieran chuckles at the memory of the early rejection.

'I played lots of solo gigs, acoustic nights and stuff but I was looking for a band to join. I joined a metal band but that didn't go too well. It wasn't really my thing and I found it hard to know what my thing was. Then I saw an ad in the paper: there was a school band that had played a school show.' The band included Ross and some friends from school, Paul and Dave. 'I went along and played them a couple of songs and the lads thought I was good, so the next week I started playing with them.'

One day Níal came down to see them practise: ' Níal lives only two doors down from Ross and he and I sat out on the step and I had a cigarette and I was like: what kind of bands do you like? and he said, "I like the Pixies and Sonic Youth," and I said, "*I* like the Pixies and Sonic Youth!"' re-enacts Kieran in an excited voice.

'And then we scored the shit out of one another!' jokes Níal. The two break into fits of laughter as they remember their first meeting and early musical 'click'. Kieran continues: 'Then I said, "Oh really, do you play in bands?" and he was like, "Yeah, I used to play with Ross, I play bass." Then Paul [bass player] didn't turn up for practice the next week and I was like, "I love Níal! Can Níal be in the band?"

'The fact was that I was hanging round purely because I wanted to play with them,' confesses Níal. 'You know, turning up wearing my Pixies T-shirt...'

'Loads of little serendipitous things happened,' Kieran recalls of their coming together.

Their first gig was part of a battle of a bands event that Kieran was organising. It was Dave, Kieran, Ross and Níal but the line-up was soon to change again.

'Dave was the loveliest fella you'd ever meet but a lot into metal. I think that we were on slightly different wavelengths.

We went in to record and the recording was rushed and it didn't work out well. Dave had a full-time job and a girlfriend and we were all like – "What the hell is a girl?" laughs Kieran. 'We were like, "Bands are great!" and loved spending all our time with it. He didn't have the time and it was not going the way that we wanted it to go. So Dave said, "Look lads, I can't really do it any more," and we said, "Grand."'

They were playing as a three-piece for a while and playing in other bands as well.

'It was one of those things. You always say in your first band you learn how to be in a band and that was kind of what it was like,' explains Nial. 'We'd done all the crap gigs: the basement gigs and the ones where you pay to play.' They had even been given a littering fine for their flyers. 'It was a real baptism of fire.'

Ross was filling in, playing drums in the band Ronan played in, Business. 'It was Ro and two of the lads from Director,' explains Kieran. 'So we all went to see the gigs. It was funny because Ross had been in school with Ro and then when they went to college, Nial was in school with Ro, so our paths were crossing. When Dave left, we were like, "What do you wanna do? Will we ask this fella who's left Business?"'

Ross thought Ro would be perfect and asked him but he said, 'No', he wasn't really interested in being in another band: he wanted to do it on his own and be a songwriter. They thought that he would change his mind if he played with them.

'Me and Kieran decided that we'd meet up with him and have a chat and see if we could persuade him. By persuade him we mean get him really, really drunk and get him to agree at the end of the night and that's exactly what we did!' laughs Nial. 'We took him out to Eamon Dorans and we got him hammered.'

Ronan had agreed only to do 'Hoot Night' with them, a night run by Thomas Dunning based on an idea he had brought over with him from Chicago, during which bands perform a song by the chosen artists of the night, in light competition, like the Cure versus the Beatles.

'It was great fun,' says Kieran. 'Then we started writing our own stuff and all a sudden it all started to click.'

'We never really broached the subject with Ro, whether he was actually in the band or not,' remembers Níal. 'We just never gave him the opportunity to say "No."'

A summer in Chicago solidified the line-up: Delorentos were complete, with the 'The' in their name having been dropped along the way. 'It's great to have a name that is unique,' says Kieran. 'We never wanted to have a name like the Spoons or the Cabbages or the something that was already something else.'

'In saying that, we lost Delorentos.com pretty quickly to another site,' grins Níal. 'A site of a more adult nature it would seem...'

Things started to progress and the band moved from having one lead singer to having a natural rotation: Kieran would play lead guitar when Ro was singing and vice versa. 'We rotate everything,' says Kieran proudly. 'For the new album, Níal sings a song, Ross sings a song: Anyone can write, anyone can do whatever they want. We wanted it to be totally free, anything goes: we didn't want to constrain it.'

It wasn't hard to get gigs: they were keen and Kieran was good at pushing to get them. They played the Ballroom of Romance and a weekday headline in Whelans and then they were offered a tour with the Flaws. Kieran had been in college with the Flaws' front man Paul Finn. They had both studied computers. 'We were trying to get a tour going and then they said, "Well, we're going to be doing this tour," so it kind of amalgamated. We alternated headline slots.'

'We did it by getting trains and buses with all our guitars because none of us drove. It was kind of deadly in hindsight,' says Níal

It was the first real insight Delorentos got into how things worked in the business, seeing A&R men show up for gigs [to see the Flaws] and so on. They cringe when they think back on one of their performances in Galway. 'We looked ridiculous, we acted like idiots, and it was a steep learning curve,' admits Níal.

The boys had beers on stage and Kieran asked, "Does anyone have a bottle opener?" and Níal went out into the crowd to get one.'

"It was really stupid,' says Níal. 'For us, that was really important because, as far as gigs go, we realised quite quickly that you can't act like a stupid college band. Like it or not, you're putting on a show, it's "showbusiness": you have to do it right. If *you* think you're an idiot, you can't blame other people for agreeing with you.'

The band started to work really hard at their shows and played every gig they could. They recorded their first EP, *Leave It On,* with Mark Carolan.

Around that time Kieran noticed a college gig in UCD that he applied for but he wasn't really paying attention as they were playing everything and anything they could at that time. It turned out to be a battle of the bands competition, something they were not keen on: 'A lot of those "pay to play" or "battle of the bands" things are an absolute sham,' says Níal.

They ended up playing the gig anyway and getting to the final stage. After their performance a nice A&R man came up to them saying positive, encouraging things. He was Barry O'Donoghue from Sony. 'It was all fantasy world stuff,' remembers Kieran.

Delorentos stayed in the competition and went through the semi-finals. Then it was the finals. To the band's surprise they ended up winning the National Student Music Awards (NSMA) and were going to be flown to London to play a gig for the NSMA UK. It was all very exciting.

They started to get interest from people before they went to London. Barry had offered them a development deal and offered to pay for some demos but the boys didn't really understand the offer and were nervous that it had strings attached. Barry asked Hugh Murray, an A&R manager for Sony UK, to meet them to explain what was on offer and talk them through it (a meeting that would pay off for them later).

'We went over to England to represent Ireland,' explains Nial. 'There was a Welsh band, a Scottish band, an English band and us. That night, was by far the biggest learning curve that we could have come across because it was the first time we were shown the aggressive, underhand side of the record industry.'

'We played the gig, we played very well and it was good fun. Then the other bands went on and everyone went mental because there were loads of people there,' continues Kieran

Then Kieran was approached after the gig by a couple of fellows and told that they had won the competition. He was on his own at the time, Ronan was being interviewed by TG4 in Irish and the others were somewhere else: 'He said "You've won the full prize. NSMA UK and Ireland final, you've won it" I was like, "Holy shit!" Then he said "I'm going to introduce you to this guy.'' This guy had his own record label and was saying, "Come upstairs and we'll talk to you." So I went upstairs and it ended up, fifteen minutes later, with this super-aggressive drunk guy from the label

shouting at me. He had a rolled-up contract in his pocket and he was like, "You have to sign the fucking contract! This is what you do. This is part of the deal! You have to sign the fucking contract or you won't get the f**king prize!"'

'I was sitting there going, "I'm really sorry but I have to talk to the rest of the band." Then two other lads he was working with came in and were standing beside me and I was fucking *freaked* out. I was saying, "No, thanks very much, no. I can't do it. I'm going to talk to the rest of the band. So I went downstairs and I met Nial and I told him what had happened. Nial was like "Holy Shit!" Then there was the prizegiving. There were people booing, the fans of the others guys, cameras were filming and we were just completely freaked out. The man continued his threats and intimidation after the award ceremony with classics like, "Oh, I'll fucking ruin you!" and, "You'll never work in this town again!!"'

'It was mad!' says Kieran, shaking his head. 'We'd just won this huge prize and we were really, really happy.' The prize included great things like recording time in Grouse Lodge, mastering in Abbey Road and an appearance on *CD:UK*.

'One of the five things was that this guy would put your single out but he was nothing to do with the actual event,' says Kieran. 'The people from NSMA Ireland were very lovely people and I would never say anything bad about them – they were just legends and everybody else involved in the event were decent people.'

'We told Hugh what had happened (he had been helping us but he wasn't managing us yet) and he was like, "All right, I've got a friend who's a lawyer. Bring this fella in and we'll have a chat with him about it." The lawyer was brilliant and tore the man to shreds.' He is now Delorentos' lawyer while Hugh, who had planned to leave Sony, became their manager.

IN BLOOM - DELORENTOS

Organised, independent and stronger from the negative experience, Delorentos formulated plans to record. They released 'Stop' as a single and then *In Love with Detail*.

The band had a list in their practice space of things they would like to do and they have managed to cross many of them off in the following months. 'There are still a few left' smiles Nial.

'I always wanted to play Electric Picnic since it started and I'd always wanted to play Oxegen. We became the first band to play both in the one year and then the next year we did it again. That's amazing to be able to do that,' says Kieran. 'We had ambitions to headline the Ambassador and we did.'

Delorentos have toured England and Italy a few times and played various showcase gigs in Canada and the USA, including twice playing the legendary SXSW festival in Austin, Texas. They go through phases of working, or having part-time jobs, but they try and make the band pay for itself. They don't pay themselves after each gig either; it all goes back into the kitty.

For *In Love with Detail* they each got a loan of €10,000 and took that as red and spent the next year paying it off: 'We didn't know how long it would take but by the time we got to the Ambassador gig, we had done it and we're very proud of that,' remarks Kieran

'As long as you cover your costs, it doesn't really matter,' says Nial. 'The whole point is to play to as many people as possible – we weren't interested in making money. You have to do it because you enjoy doing it in the first place and that's the lesson that we learned quite recently with the whole band breaking up. It many ways it was the most cathartic thing that could have happened because we all realised that the main reason we were doing this was because we enjoyed it and that it was something special.'

Delorentos had seen many brilliant bands break up so they knew how easily it could happen but they didn't ever think it would be an issue for them. 'We went on tour with the Immediate and then they broke up and we were going: "Fuck, it's such a shame!" It was the same with Life after Modelling and loads of bands that we like. They broke up and we went, "Jesus, that's not going to be us!" And all a sudden, it *was* us.'

Kieran tries to explain what happened. 'Last year [2008] was very tough. We put a lot of pressure on ourselves. We put a lot of pressure on one another and we worked very, very hard to write an album that was better, stronger and more emotional: a step on from the last one. At the same time, we were trying to release the first album in the UK. Then we played a gig in the Ambassador and A&R people came to the gig. They loved it and all a sudden, we had this interest. We still had this plan of releasing the album ourselves in the UK and we were going to tour the hell out of it. We were going to finance it ourselves and we were going to do it off our own bat. Then the label guys came in and said "If you sign to this, you can tour the world."'

The label was going to invest huge money in to the band. They were told they would be touring the world for a year. It was a dream opportunity, a chance to quit the day job. So the band put their plans to release *In Love With Detail* in the UK on hold and waited for the deal to close but it wasn't to be. 'The people wouldn't sign it because the backing fell through,' says Kieran. 'We took our eye off the ball. We didn't do what we always had done, which is, be self-sufficient; don't wait for people and don't be blinded by promises of things you don't know.'

Nial comes to their defence. 'We had been through such a long period when we were just working and working and working. We were probably more susceptible to [that kind of offer] and that's when the cracks began to show.'

'We were already really pushing ourselves to write songs. We were writing and doing extra practices and it was a tough time. We weren't playing as many gigs and we weren't doing the kind of stuff that feeds the enjoyment of it,' reflects Kieran.

Nial agrees. 'It was all a really hard slog for eighteen months or so and being really tough on one another as well. There was no allowing one another do anything else.'

They went in to record demos for the second album in November-December 2008: 'We decided to do the ones that satisfied our creativity. The eighteen songs we wrote were very different: some were slow and heavy and some very mad stuff, like *pieces*, as opposed to music,' says Kieran.

The band reached Christmas and took a couple of weeks off for the holidays. When they came back and started to practise it wasn't long before Ro said, "I can't do this any more." That was it.

'We didn't announce if for ages,' says Nial. 'There was loads of talking and an awful lot of walks on the beach or meeting in coffee shops with Ro and sitting in his house.'

For Kieran it was the realisation that: 'This thing that we'd dedicated everything to was gone. Now you're not in a band.' All the time and effort they had spent building something was now over.

'Personally, I was determined that we were going to release what we had, even if it meant just the three of us recording it,' says Nial. They agreed the songs were too strong to let go and that they were going to record them.

Kieran explains. 'We went back into Ro and said, "Look, we're going to record this album and we'd like you to be a part of it if you'd like to be? He said, "OK, I could probably do that."'

'It didn't take Ro long to realise that the worst thing for him was that we were his friends. I think he was surprised that we didn't try to beat him up,' says Nial. 'I think that it was a good thing for him to realise, that, as friends, we were more concerned that he was OK and that we were OK, as opposed to the band being OK.'

Kieran continues: 'And because we were such good friends we said, "We're not just going to let you leave and grab another member. We're going to end this together. What we're going to do is record the album together and play some gigs, say goodbye to a few people who have been so good to us and then it's over."'

They gave the tracks to producer Gareth Mannix to listen to and he was really enthusiastic. It was just what they needed to hear. 'At that stage we were kind of wondering whether the whole thing had been a waste of time and whether it was even any good,' admits Nial.

The pre-production for the album was awkward to begin with: 'Gareth came out to practise an awful lot during that period and he just sat there drinking beer and making suggestions. He was brilliant because his attitude was, "I don't care about what's going on. You four people are a band that I'm working with and as far as I am concerned, there's no problem and if there is a problem, it's not mine to deal with. I'm here to make this sound as good as possible." It was deadly because it took the bullshit out of it,' says Nial.

In the meantime Kieran had been writing. Music is a way for him to say how he is feeling: 'I wrote a song about the break-up of the band and it's one of the saddest things I've ever written. We said that it was going to be the last track on the album and the last thing everyone was going to hear. We're so proud of it.'

From the day they started recording the album they loved it. Doing the album was the fun part, the part that they had been working towards for a year and a half. Close to the end of recording, Ro started expressing doubts about what he was doing – whether he wanted to leave or not.

'We'd already decided in February [2009] to announce to everybody that we'd broken up,' reminds Kieran. 'It got to April and Ro came back and met with us and said "I'm very sorry about what happened. Would you accept me back in the band?"'

'We had to think about it. What were people going to say? It comes back to the thing we've always said: "There's no rules." You can do whatever the fuck you want. We decided to do it,' says Kieran.

Being honest is very important to the band, having been through what they have, so they decided the best thing was for Ro to write a letter explaining the decision to their fans and they posted it on their websites.

The band announced that they would be staying together and releasing their second album *You Can Make Sound* in the autumn. 'You Can Make Sound', the single, was released as a free download in May 2009, followed by a tour. What was going to be a goodbye tour became a celebration instead. The band was overwhelmed by the positive reaction it got. It was the most enjoyable tour they had done to date.

Kieran smiles: 'A girl sent an email saying, "I love *You Can Make Sound*! I have it downloaded and I have it up as a loud as I can on my iPod and I walk around listening to it all day." 'That means way more then getting paid for a gig.'

The second single, 'S.e.c.r.e.t.', followed on 2 October with a video by Eoghan Kidney. *You Can Make Sound* was mixed by Cenzo Townsend, Adrian Bushby and Phil Hayes and released on Delorecords on 9 October 2009. It was followed by an extensive national tour throughout October and November.

Speaking of the new album, Níal says 'The four of us are really proud of how it sounds and how it stands next to the first one. I think, more and more, we're becoming the kind of band that we want to be.'

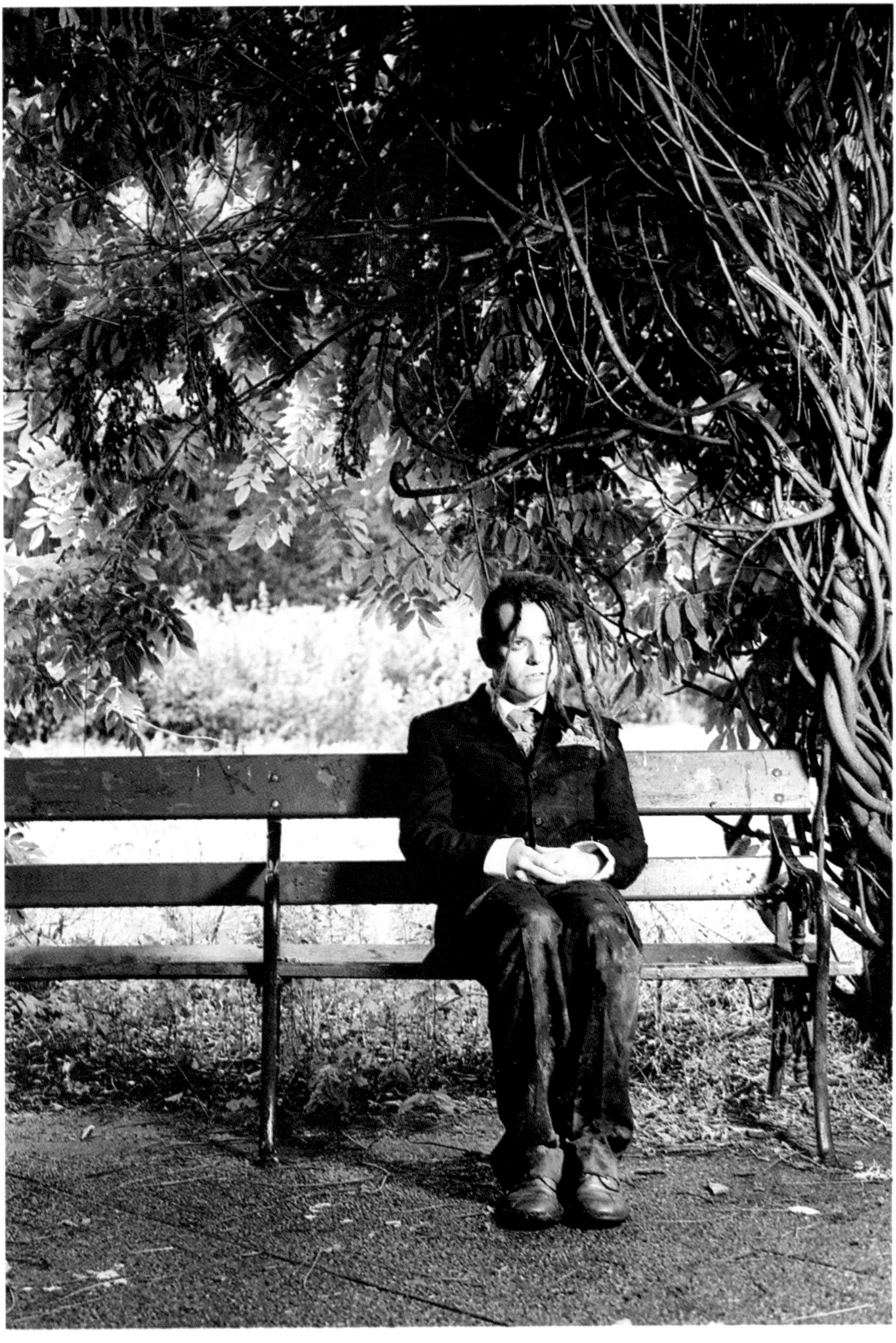

Duke Special

Artist
Duke Special
(Peter Wilson)

Albums
Adventures in Gramophone
(the two EPs)
Songs from the Deep Forest
Orchestral Manoeuvres in
Belfast (live album)
I Never Thought This
Day Would Come

EPs
Lucky Me
My Villain Heart
Your Vandal

Label
Universal Music

Management
Phil Nelson and Fran Moore at
First Column Management

Websites
www.dukespecial.com
www.MySpace.com/dukespecial

Duke Special is a lovely, genuine, gentle man with a warmth and sincerity that are all too rare.

He sings with his Northern accent intact and has a romantic, theatrical style that has set him apart from other 'alternative' musicians. Years of hard work and constant touring have built him a large, loyal fan base. He has an enviable, constant creativity; one that directs itself as much to theatre and other areas of art as it does to music.

Duke Special has enjoyed extensive daytime radio support and has sold out numerous Irish and UK tours. He has supported some of the biggest names in music, having played with Van Morrison, Snow Patrol, Crowded House and Duffy. He won a Meteor Award for Best Irish Male in 2009 and has twice been shortlisted for the Choice Music Prize; first for *Adventures in Gramophone* in 2005 and again for *Songs from the Deep Forest* in 2006.

He has played all sizes of venue; from the O2 Academy in London and Vicar Street in Dublin to the Spirit Store in Dundalk. Not only has Duke Special played the big festivals in Ireland such as Oxegen and Electric Picnic but he has created his own arts festival, Dukebox.

Duke Special has also taken to the stage with the acclaimed actress Fiona Shaw, cast in Deborah Warner's National Theatre production of Bertolt Brecht's *Mother Courage and Her Children* at the Olivier in London.

Duke Special grew up in Downpatrick in Northern Ireland with three older sisters, all whom were into music. 'They all played piano and sang and my mother played piano and her mother was a piano teacher, so the piano was very much part of the furniture, part of the household. From an early age I remember doing musical collaborations with my sisters. I suppose, musically, in their record collection it was the Beatles, Neil Young, Dylan and folk music.'

He grew up going to church and singing in choirs. 'As a child, when you're growing up, whatever music is around gets under your skin without your even realising, and that sense of melody and communal singing has always stayed with me. Like the Christmas family get-togethers when we and our cousins would be mortified into playing our current exam pieces or whatever little song we had learnt for something or other. That kind of got you over the stage nerves. To this day playing in front of family is still the most nerve-racking thing!' laughs Duke. 'Music was just a part of the vocabulary, really.'

Duke had been taking piano lessons from the age of seven and his sisters always encouraged him to write when he was young.

'When I was about twelve or thirteen a guy showed me how to play chords on the piano by following guitar chords, as opposed to following music, which I had been. That opened up a whole world where I could start playing a lot of direct chords and trying to learn by ear.'

Duke Special received career advice in school but the options presented to him for music were very limited. 'I think they were really ignorant as to what was possible and they just said, "You could become a teacher or do a music degree," so there weren't the same options as there are now. Also, growing up in Northern Ireland, there wasn't a huge number of role models: you had Van Morrison and the Undertones and Sticky Fingers but they all seemed untouchable and kind of beyond what you could ever imagine doing or being. Way too cool for a piano player! Piano wasn't a very cool instrument in those days,' laughs Duke.

'When I left school, I was saving up to go to Canada to performance arts college there and instead I ended up joining a band in England for two years.'

The band was not trying to get signed, they were touring around playing youth clubs: essentially, community youth work.

'It was the only thing that I came across that I remotely wanted to do. So I did that for two years, then came home to Belfast and went to university to do this community youth work as a degree but as soon as I started it, I felt all I could think about was music,' says Duke.

'I started playing with a guy from Belfast called Brian Houston, who is like a mixture of Dylan, Elvis, Kris Kristofferson, Van Morrison and Springsteen all rolled into one. I played piano with him off and on for two or three years and that was my proper apprenticeship. I realised this *is* really possible. He was blazing a trail for me and for a lot of other people who were trying to make a go of it. So then I played in a couple of different bands before striking out on my own as Duke Special [2001].'

'I was writing but the songs weren't great, to be honest. Gradually I was being mentored by records that I was buying,' says Duke. 'Suddenly, they were opening up whole new worlds to me like Tom Waits, Nick Cave, Aimée Mann, Elliot Smith, people like that. I was suddenly really listening to the music and listening to the songwriting. Then there was a band from the North called the Amazing Pilots (Paul Pilot, who produced my last two records). He was a big inspiration to me and that band also, for doing something really interesting and not the normal kind of rock indie band, or rock metal band – which seemed to be the only route.'

'All those were formative years for me, really. I wasn't one of these guys who at the age of seventeen had the whole package,' admits Duke. 'I was definitely on a journey, and still am, I suppose. Then I was on a journey of finding my voice and learning to embrace the piano and realising that actually just because you are not very current or the particular cool sound or the Zeitgeist of the year doesn't mean anything. I was learning how to be an artist.'

'Then when I recorded some demos with Paul, I didn't have a name for what I was doing. I wanted the name to represent something about the sound that was intriguing and enigmatic – not just my own name, because I love the way bands have names and it's almost like a part of their identity. Solo artists can sometimes just seem boy-next-door, playing a few tunes. I wanted to be something more theatrical,' explains Duke

'Once I had created the *Lucky Me* EP, I had to consider how I would perform that live, because there was drums and gramophone crackle on the EP from beginning to end,' says Duke. 'I watched a film about the life of Andy Kaufmann – *Man on the Moon*. In that he had a little record player and I thought that would be great, but maybe a gramophone. So I started accompanying myself with a gramophone. I had backing tracks playing on that or little spoken-word albums from the early-1900s, like lectures about blood and its parts or germs and the spread of bacteria. And I'd play little snippets of things during songs or as little interludes and I started touring, doing these little supports all around Ireland, England, Scotland, Wales.'

'I realised I don't want to sit around for records labels to go, "Yes, you're good," or, "You're not good," so the plan was just to go out and start playing. I started playing support; driving to Dundalk and playing support in the Spirit Store for someone who had like eight people there; and playing for no money. Then I would go and play in Mallow or Clonakilty or Galway, all on the same kind of deal. I was living off whatever CDs I could sell of that first EP.'

Duke Special was starting to build a fan base through hard work and constant touring. Between tours he was playing in bars in Belfast and he started to get more high-profile support slots. 'There was a whole range of things that were probably little step-ups, support tours with Aqualung in England, Hal, Bell X1 – those kinds of things in Ireland and in England. That really helped.'

My Villain Heart, Duke Special's second EP, was released in 2004. Shortly after that, Duke Special met his manager, who had the idea of combining his two EPS and making them into one album. Having an album meant greater profile and album reviews, so *Lucky Me* and *My Villain Heart* became *Adventures in Gramophone* in 2005.

Positive press abounded and radio playlisted 'Last Night I Nearly Died (But I Woke Up Just in Time)' and 'Freewheel'. *Adventures in Gramophone* was then shortlisted for the inaugural Choice Music Prize Irish Album of the Year – to the surprise of Duke: 'Suddenly I was playing in front of all the major press in Ireland. I was on the radar: it was great.'

'Then I did a third EP [*Your Vandal*],' says Duke. 'All these EPs I recorded with very, very little money and most of the music was recorded above a tanning salon near where I live. For the second EP we had hardly any budget and we recorded the drums from the sound of wardrobe doors closing and hitting a bodhrán with the side of a stick, just to make clicky sounds. The third EP was recorded on even less. We cannibalised drum tracks from the previous EPs and I played trumpet on it and a little pump organ. So they were very much little labours of love,' says Duke. 'If that was all I had ever done and I had stayed at that level, I would be loving it still.'

'Then I got a publishing deal in London. A guy came to hear someone else play and ended up staying for me and signing me to Nettwerk Publishing,' says Duke. Nettwerk is the independent label and management company created around Canadian singer Sarah McLoughlin.

'They had a publishing arm and I signed to that. And through that, through my management and a number of other avenues, we came to the attention of a label in England called V2, at that stage home of Elbow, Paul Weller, Bloc Party and Ron Sexsmith. It was just a really good, large independent label.'

Record labels are only ever as good as their staff, and Duke was lucky that V2 had a new boss.

'I'd actually been for a meeting with the head of the record label before but it was a different guy. I waited all day for a meeting and then he said,

"I have to go now, I'm really sorry," and I was so disillusioned. This was my second time going back here but it was a different guy – a guy called Charlie Pinder. He sat me down and said, "I don't know why you haven't been signed before, I love the stuff. It's unusual what you are doing but I think with the team you have around you we can really do something with this." I nearly cried because it was like "at last!" As much as you believe in what you are doing yourself and the people around you believe in you, it's such a boost to have your peers or a label go, "This is great. You deserve to be signed. Let's take it on to another level."'

It was the validation that Duke Special needed. 'At the same time it was still a hand-to-mouth kind of existence and a well-meaning family going, "So how long are you going to do this for before you settle down and get a real job?" Because I had family by this stage, I wasn't seventeen or eighteen with no responsibilities. I had to make it work.'

'Anybody who was involved in music saw that there was something that I was doing that was working but there is so much in those early days which is about prospecting. You are doing tours and you are not really making any money, whereas my contemporaries were earning a packet in well-paid jobs!' laughs Duke. 'Sometimes I was going, "What am I doing here?" But I knew that I couldn't stop. I'd come to the conclusion that I was an artist. Whether I was going to be a well-off artist or not was no longer an issue, I knew this was something I'm going to do for the rest of my life,' says Duke.

'That was such a joy, such a relief. The pressure completely went. I realised it's not about getting a record deal, it's about making art that I am really proud of, that I feel is what I want to say. It took the pressure off trying to be current and trying to find what would work on radio. Suddenly it was about, "I'm a songwriter and a performer and that's not going to go away."'

IN BLOOM - DUKE SPECIAL

It's the sort of realisation that often comes with age and Duke doesn't disagree: 'Although Duke Special is only twenty-eight; still is and has been for quite a few years!' he laughs, 'Peter Wilson probably realised that at about thirty!' It's one of the bonuses of creating a character; characters never age. I can get away with a little bit less than what I am but I'm certainly not twenty-eight any more. I like the idea that when I'm seventy, it will still be on press releases, "Twenty-eight year old Duke Special," and I'll be seeing interviewers' eyebrows rise,' laughs Duke.

Songs from the Deep Forest came out on V2 records in September 2006. It too was shortlisted for the Choice Music Prize and Duke Special was nominated for Best Irish Male at the 2007 Meteor Awards.

Duke Special then signed to Universal Records when V2 was bought over. His third album *I Never Thought This Day Would Come* came out in October 2008 on Universal and had an instant radio hit with the lead single 'Sweet, Sweet Kisses'. He was nominated for Best Irish Male at the Meteor Awards 2009 for the second time and won. 'Why Does Anybody Love' was released to radio in the summer during festival season, before Duke's inaugural festival in August: DUKEBOX.

Duke Special Presents DUKEBOX took place in Custom House Square in Belfast, as part of Belfast's Belsonic '09, with the Magic Numbers, Bell X1, David Kitt, Jerry Fish & the Mudbug Club and Panama Kings amongst the musicians performing. It was created by Duke to be an annual arts festival, something he is very proud of and excited about: 'It's people that I've discovered as I've been touring, from different countries; people whose music I really love; art, theatre and children's area. I think next year it's going to be in the Folk and Transport Museum.'

With all the touring, EPs, albums and family life you would think that Duke Special was too busy for extra projects but he seems to thrive on them.

'I love the variety. I genuinely love doing an album campaign in which I have to go out and plug a new record and try to sell out venues and tour. I've done a lot of one-off projects, like I recently curated a night of music which I wrote based on silent movies from the 1930s and 1940s from Germany and Eastern Europe. I did a night called the *Silhouette Old Time Mystery Radio Show* where I commissioned a three-act play to be written by a friend of mine from Chicago and it was set like a radio noir play with live actors making sound effects and house bands and singers all singing songs about crime and murder. I recently recorded an EP about the life of Huckleberry Finn – five songs by Kurt Weill. It's from an unfinished musical of *Huckleberry Finn* (he died before it was finished). For the most recent record [*I Never Thought This Day Would Come*] I recorded twelve songs based on the life of a silent movie star, Hector Mann, who disappeared under mysterious circumstances in the 1920s.

'I read a book about him and wrote one song based on one of his movies and I realised there wasn't enough time – the recording was imminent – so I sent the book to eleven other writers – Neil Hannon, Ed Harcourt, Paul Pilot and eight other writers – and they each sent me back one song which had to be in the style of pre-rock'n'roll, and then I recorded all twelve songs over three days with Steve Albini in Chicago. So I love those kinds of things which aren't just playing the industry game or the cycle of: record an album, tour, do radio, stop, record an album, do radio, stop. So that's something that has really appealed to me. '

There have been many highlights in Duke Special's career to date, one of which was performing on Jools Holland during the *Songs from the Deep Forest* campaign. 'I was on tour with the Divine Comedy throughout Europe and England and Ireland. So that was another important landmark, probably for perception from the outside, with people going, "Oh, no way! You were on that programme weren't you?" and also for myself going, "I was on flippin' Jools Holland with the Raconteurs, Amy Winehouse, Muse and bands like that,' says Duke.

'I did *Top Of the Pops*, although it was *Top of the Pops 2*. Jools Holland is still the one I'd definitely love to do again. That one never disappears; you kind of want to keep doing that one. I think I feel really content now, I'm not trying to make it. I feel really lucky that I've had enough success to be able to keep doing what I'm doing.'

The success that Duke Special enjoys was gradual: with every tour and album he built and added another layer. All well as supporting other artists, his own headline shows have taken in venues as diverse as Cyprus Avenue in Cork, Róisín Dubh in Galway, Vicar Street and the O2 Academy in London. He still makes an effort to do all-ages shows, something many artists stop doing as they get bigger.

'It's brilliant in some ways [touring]. It's so satisfying. You get an immediate response to your work but it's nowhere near as glamorous as you'd expect. A lot of the shows I'm doing, you're driving in a transit van and loading in all your gear. I had to buy a ramp recently for an upright acoustic piano which I brought on tour with me. Ya know, spending four hundred pounds on a ramp isn't part of my dream!' laughs Duke. 'That isn't what I dreamt about as a teenager.'

'I find for me personally, when I was doing a tour for maybe six or seven weeks on the trot, away from home; your head goes to a weird space because that becomes normal. You are thinking about a gig that night and normal life just passes you by and you get a phone call about paying a bill or something and you are like, "I don't understand this, what *is* this conversation?" Where it seems to work for me is two or three weeks at the most and then some normal life and that seems like a good balance for me: I need those roots.'

'It's like any job, there are great bits and exciting bits and there are graft bits, which for me is the writing, where you've got to kind of nine-to-five it. The inspiration is in there somewhere but you've got to put yourself in a round with a blank page and a piano and *work*. To get to the good stuff, you've got to go through the uninspired parts and writing really shit lyrics and really shit melodies and then you come back the next day and improve it a little bit and gradually it's getting there. Then occasionally you get a song and it just pops out and it's often the most successful one but a lot of the time you've just got to put in the hours but that's exciting as well, because I'm listening to records while I'm doing that or reading poetry or reading plays or going to see art. Just trying to have all your sensors open to inspiration.'

'I love what I do and I feel really lucky to be able to devote a lot of time to writing and to creating. I think for that reason as well, I want them to be really good, to kind of justify the fact I have a really good job.'

'It's not a case of you either become an overnight success or it's nothing. I think it's so entirely possible for it to be a journey and for things to grow and change and develop and get better.' It's his belief in development, in private as well as public growth, that is behind Duke Special's aversion to shows like *Pop Idol* and *X Factor*. 'I think it's a catastrophic mistake for a lot of people to go that route and it's maybe not as glamorous or as sexy doing it the long slog but artistically, it's way better I think.'

Duke Special has many exciting creative projects on the go and planned for the future. One of them came about from his performance at 'Oscar Wilde: Honouring the Irish in Film' pre-Academy Awards party put on by the US-Ireland Alliance in LA. Duke Special performed at the after-show and made a big impression on Fiona Shaw. She made contact with him via the organisers and came to see him perform.

'She came along to the duet I did with Neil Hannon in Vicar Street with her director, Deborah Warner. They are doing a production of *Mother Courage*, a Bertolt Brecht play, in the National Theatre in London and they were wondering if I would be interested in writing the music for it but also to be in the play as a kind of singing narrator, some sort of Greek chorus. So that's what I'm going to be doing from September to December [2009]; sixty-five performances of *Mother Courage* with Fiona Shaw in the National Theatre! It's going to be *unbelievable*,' says Duke

'I'm doing it as Duke Special, so it's a bit of a left turn, in that I'm not going to be touring in that time but it's something I've always tried to do; bring theatrical devices into my shows. I'm actually more excited about that than any record deal; because creatively it's going to be so, so satisfying and I'm intrigued about where that will go and what doors it will open.'

'For me it's about growing and always moving as an artist and not just doing the same thing over and over and over again. Any of my heroes – Tom Waits, Nick Cave – theatre is always something they've been involved in; it's where the arts collide that it gets really interesting. I think that's where it really excites me. The idea of getting up and singing songs is great but I love the idea of it being something more than that, of it being an experience and being able to put a frame on the songs so it actually gives it some context. I'm thrilled to be doing that.'

'I think with theatre, the audience comes with that expectation and that willingness to believe and to be involved in the play, so there's a real energy in that. Music is like acting as well; every time you do a song you have to get under the skin of it again to make it believable.'

As for a new album, it won't be long but it will be preceded or followed by any number of fantastic creative projects that Duke Special has been dreaming up.

'I'm really keen to stage the Hector Mann songs in a play. Also just to keep writing. I'd love to bring the album out in the springtime of next year, [2010] but maybe record the *Mother Courage* stuff... Who knows!'

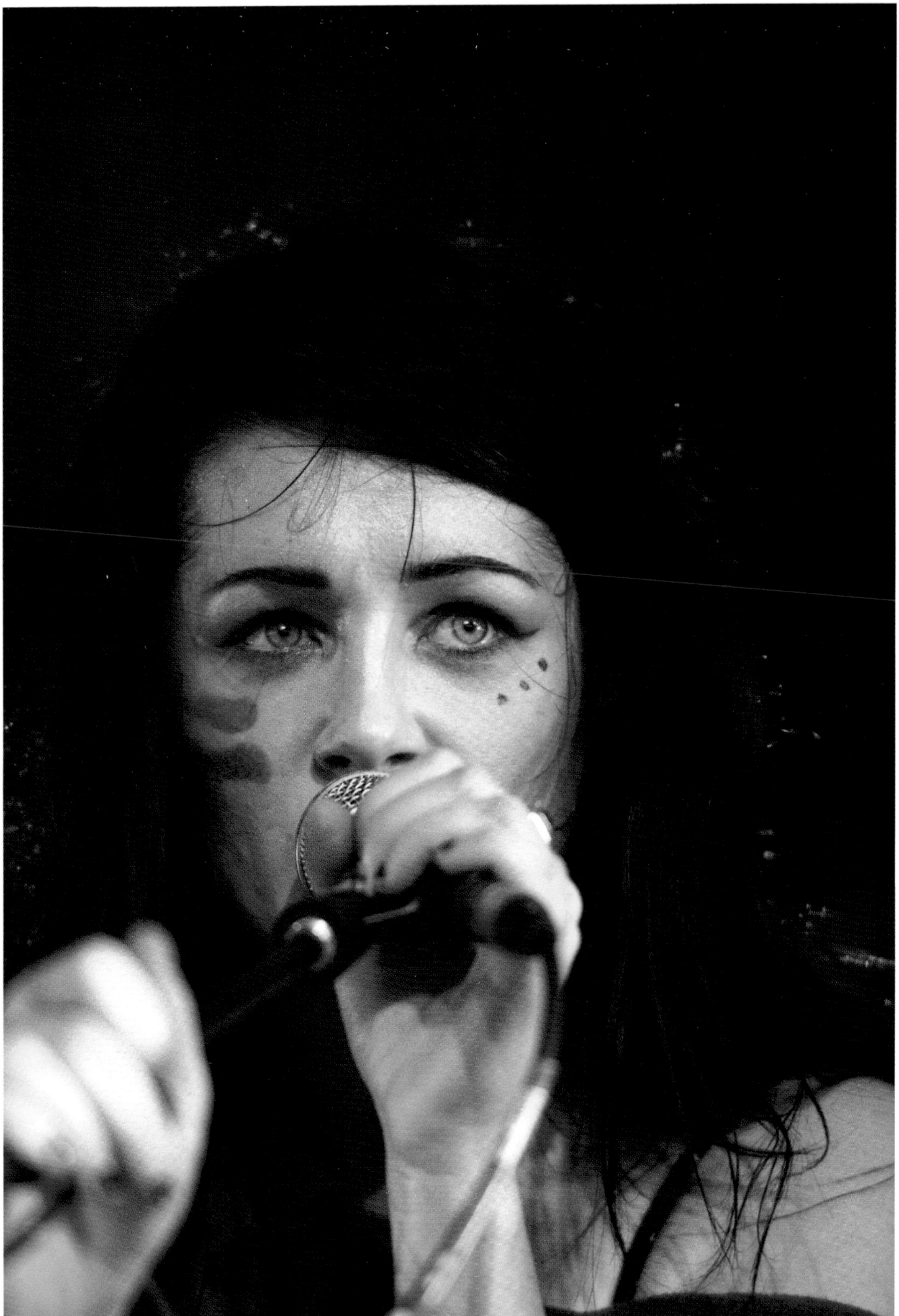

Fight Like Apes

Band Members
MayKay
(Mary-Kate Geraghty)
Pockets (Jamie Fox)
Tom Ryan
Adrian Mullan

Albums
*Fight Like Apes and the Mystery
of the Golden Medallion*
*Fight Like Apes and the Mystery
of the Golden Medallion*
(festival edition w/bonus disc)

EPs
*How Am I Supposed to Kill You if
You Have All the Guns?*
*David Carradine Is a Bounty
Hunter Whos Robotic Arm
Hates Your Crotch*
Jake Summers EP
*You Filled His Head with Fluffy
Clouds and Jolly Ranchers.
What Did You Think Was Going
to Happen?*

Label
Model Citizen Records

Management
Niall Muckian, Rubyworks

Websites
www.fightlikeapesmusic.com
www.MySpace.com/fightlikeapesmusic

*MAYKAY AND POCKETS WERE PRESENT
FOR THE INTERVIEW. (POCKETS REFERS
TO MAYKAY AS MARY AND MAYKAY
REFERS TO POCKETS AS JAMIE).*

Fight like Apes are hilarious. They are exceptionally hard-working, intelligent, cheeky, mischievous, *lovely* brats. They are as much fun as you could hope for in a group of individuals. MayKay is a rare talent; a sassy front woman, singer and writer. Combine this with Pockets' writing and music and you have a creative force to be reckoned with – add Adrian and Tom and you have one of the coolest bands ever to have come out of Ireland. A high-profile musician once said in an interview: 'I am so glad Fight Like Apes came along, I think the Irish music scene really needed them,' and their fans agree.

Fight Like Apes (or FLApes) make brilliant synth pop with punk attitude, high-energy, catchy, edgy, songs about everything from ex-boyfriends to nursery rhymes. Singles 'Jake Summers', 'Lend Me Your Face', 'Tie Me Up With Jackets' and 'Something Global' all received extensive alternative radio play and music press. They have been nominated for five Meteor Awards (Best Irish Band, Best Irish Live Performance 2008, Best Irish Band, Best Irish Live Performance, Best Irish Album 2009) and were shortlisted for the Choice Music Prize Irish Album of the Year 2008. They have played the festival circuit numerous times, including Glastonbury, Oxegen, T in the Park, Benicassim, Pukkelpop and Reading. Their début album, *Fight Like Apes and the Mystery of the Golden Medallion*, has been released in Ireland, the UK, Benelux, Australia and Japan and they have released an EP in North America.

MayKay and Pockets met on holiday in Spain. Pockets was friends with MayKay's older sister and MayKay had been told she should meet him when she was there.

'I was in Mount Sackville secondary school in Chapelizod and he was in Castleknock College, and they are a two-minute walk from each other,' explains MayKay of the connection. 'I didn't want to go away, none of my friends were going to be there and I was meeting all these annoying people. I met Jamie who was, as far as I remember, just insulting everyone. At first I though he was really rude and then I was like, "I was just going to say that! I was thinking the same thing!"'

The pair soon hit it off, as her sister expected. 'We hung out in this bar called Ribera [in Spain] that played Kerrang and Magic,' recalls MayKay.

'A perfect balance between metal and power pop,' interjects Pockets.

'He made me write on a tissue in the bar that I would be involved in musical exploits only with him,' laughs MayKay. 'He had never even heard me sing!'

'No, that was really stupid of me!' admits Pockets.

Thinking back on that time, MayKay admits that she was not into alternative music yet (MayKay was fifteen and Pockets was seventeen): 'I was into music but I was into pop music. I knew certain things like the Eurythmics that my mum listened to; some Patti Smith and the Rolling Stones and stuff – but that was all I knew of alternative music,' says MayKay.

'I was in bands in school, I mean, nothing serious,' says Pockets. 'I had just come out of a band and wasn't really looking to do anything at all. I just sort of decided that me and Mary were gonna make music, even though I didn't really know if she could sing or not!'

Pockets was doing Music for his Leaving Cert and he wanted a girl to accompany him and sing on his Leaving cert practical exam (guitar and piano). Even though he had not heard her sing, he asked MayKay. 'We were going to do Richard Marks's "Right Here Waiting",' grins MayKay. 'We were going to really melt the judges' hearts but we didn't get around to doing that – which is a disaster!' she laughs. 'The first time I went to sing with him I was so nervous. I sang in school choirs and stuff successfully, to the point that I didn't get kicked out; I was a soprano in the choir, lead in the school play (well the lead male!); I am sure I could hold a note but I am sure it probably made you nervous [to Pockets] because I was nervous,' confesses MayKay.

'Yeah, you were quite shy about singing. Which is quite odd considering what you are like now,' laughs Pockets. 'It was bizarre because I didn't know she was really good at the start', he confesses, 'It took me a few weeks: it took a friend of mine to say, "You know, she's amazing," and I was like, "Really? I know she's good – but *really*?" and he was like, "No, seriously, she's incredible, she has an incredible voice."'

'It was amazing for me because I was fifteen, hanging out in the boys' school rehearsing for this,' laughs MayKay. 'Amazing! You have no idea how much fake tan I wore either: *total junkie*, like don't worry if anyone else has make-up on, I have enough for everyone! It was sick, it was horrific!' she says, still laughing.

'I had blonde hair,' reveals Pockets sheepishly after MayKay's confession. 'Short blonde hair.'

'We were effectively the biggest sell-outs of all time!' laughs MayKay.

Pockets and MayKay continued to play together in various bands throughout school. 'We went in and out of some questionable bands,' says Pockets. 'This one band in particular lasted about two years. We didn't even know what a DI [digital input] was at that stage: how to plug in for a gig. We needed to learn things like that. We would go to venues and just sort of scratch our heads trying to pretend we knew what we were doing. It took us about two years to learn how to be in a band.'

'And I was, dare I say it, timid,' says MayKay.

Pockets nods, in agreement. 'Yeah, very timid.'

Pockets reckons that Mary's role in the band was exactly what people expected of girls at the time: to sing harmonies and make somebody else look good. Musically they were not able to fully express themselves either. 'We would try to add some distortion or some samples and stuff but

that was regarded as too left-field. Eventually we split up and we went one way and the lead singer went the other way,' explains Pockets. 'We are still really good friends with them: we just wanted completely different types of music.'

They came up with the name that very night. 'We are going to start a band called Fight Like Apes!' remembers MayKay. 'The name was so important – I don't know why other bands are so casual about it because it says so much.'

Fight Like Apes was the opposite to all the other bands they had been in before. The name *itself* felt like the antithesis of the others.

'It was turmoil as opposed to safety,' explains Pockets. 'The other band was really, really safe music and just unchallenging. So the idea was to create a band that was as angry as we felt at the time and Fight Like Apes seemed like the perfect name for it. We didn't know what kind of music we were going to make but Fight Like Apes sounded to us like something we wanted to be involved in.'

They got the name from a friend, Sean Mahon: 'Sean wanted to call his band that, but the boys in the Ghostwood Project said, "No way." So we stole it!' jokes Pockets. 'I rang him and said, "We were going to call our band that," and he said, "Somebody should!" He doesn't seem to mind: they have all been amazingly supportive and happy for us since then.'

With a name and a vision, writing came quickly and easily. 'We kind of had that splurge; we hadn't been writing without boundaries for a long time,' says Pockets. 'You had to keep within the realm, no non-sequiturs; "What is that? You can't write about toast in a song!" So it was an absolute splurge of stuff that I had been building up for ages. I had already been making some music and Mary said, "I have some lyrics for that," so we did "Do You Karate?", "Jake Summers", "Lend Me

Your Face", "Battle Stations" and "Lumpy Dough", all in a few weeks. It came so easily.'

When it comes to writing, Pockets and MayKay tend to bounce ideas off each other. 'I find it very difficult to write without him,' says MayKay. 'If I write a song it ends up being my work at the end of it but I wouldn't OK it by myself – you kind of need someone there. Like if I go, "Oh that's ridiculous!" He would say, "Yeah, it is but it's good ridiculous!"'

'Often anyone's best ideas need encouragement because it's going to be on the edge if it's a good idea in the first place and generally when an idea is on the edge, you are not going to want to show it to someone; so it's best always to bounce,' says Pockets.

Yeah,' agrees MayKay, 'because we are both as honest as we are nice to each other, in equal measure.'

Fight Like Apes were already a four-piece; they had been messing around together already for years: 'Tom was in school with Pockets and Adrian came about just because we were looking for a drummer to jam with and we were on a forum and he was looking for a band,' says MayKay.

Before Fight Like Apes played their first gig they rehearsed for ages: 'We wanted a ready-made band. What a lot of bands do is just kind of stumble out there and grow up in public – we didn't want to grow up in public,' says Pockets. 'We had six songs and we rehearsed them to death and wouldn't talk in between. We were never going to talk, we were just going to play six songs and get off the stage,' he explains. 'And now you can't shut us up!' he laughs.

'I think, especially for me and Jamie, we knew we were going to put on a show,' says MayKay. 'I am so sick of seeing bands try and look so insanely cool that they think it's ridiculous to move or to

do anything. It wasn't going to be a rendition of an album; we weren't going to just get up on stage and play our songs; we wanted to make it something a little bit more than a gig.'

Rehearsed and ready to rock, FLApes took to the stage; the first on in a line-up of bands in Whelans. It did not go well: 'Our first gig was Whelans, on 3 November, 2006,' remembers MayKay.

'I fucking wish we hadn't played at this stage! It was terrible.' Pockets cringes at the memory.

'We were first on to about ten people all whom, bar one, though we were an absolute waste of space. We found that hilarious, though – just that childish thing of annoying people,' laughs MayKay.

'I thought that more people would get it than did,' confesses Pockets. 'It was a bit horrible. I was friends with the other bands, so they were awkward around us afterwards. I overheard friends saying, "I suppose Jamie ads a bit of a comic element to it."'

'We would be talking to people about My Bloody Valentine and At The Drive-In and they would be all excited to hear us, after listing off all these credible bands, and then we would come out on stage like a bunch of clowns!' says MayKay, thinking back.

One guy got it, though, and gave them a gig in the Mezz. It was a free Monday-night slot and they ended up playing there for weeks: learning the ropes of playing live. 'You learn about things like five-minute line checks. We started pretty much at the bottom of the barrel in terms of glamorous gigging,' says MayKay. 'That's why now at Whelans or the Ambassador I am like a kid in Disneyland.'

The band was having fun as they got better and people started to warm to them. 'After about three or four weeks, people started getting it and suddenly it wasn't just we who liked our band!' laughs Pockets

'We supported Hoovers and Sledgehammers one night in the Mezz to twenty people and this was a milestone for us because they liked us. This was a band we respected *so* much,' says MayKay. 'I think our focus shifted; it's such an underground pretentious thing to say but we were like, "If we can impress ten people that we really like and respect, we didn't really care."'

FLApes members never put pressure on one another. Even early on when they were not getting a great reaction, they prioritised enjoying it. 'I think that's why we are all still extremely close; we never fall out. We have spats, like he and I are like brother and sister [referring to Pockets], we fall out for five minutes and then one of us will go, "So, em, good gig," and we are OK again!' laughs MayKay.

'We kind of have this agreement that if one of us stops having fun they are free to go,' says Pockets.

'Certainly for me it would be too hard to tour this extensively, if you weren't having fun or weren't getting along. I wouldn't waste my life doing it,' says MayKay. 'Definitely not.'

There is a perception that FLApes burst on to the scene but it's a false one. FLApes worked their butt off, gigging up and down the country in the most unglamorous way. They had a manager, Dave Curran, who worked on booking them loads of gigs. 'He was great because at the time what we needed to do was play for anybody who would watch,' says MayKay

'We had two cars – drive, sleep wherever we could," says Pockets. 'If they would provide petrol money we would play their gig; if they wouldn't provide petrol money we would play the gig anyway!' Pockets and MayKay laugh. 'If they had a floor we would sleep on it; if they didn't we would sleep in our cars,' says Pockets.

'We had the time of our lives doing it as well. We started off sleeping in cars and stuff so now for me, honest to God, staying in Travelodges having warm water and a bed is still great,' says MayKay. 'I am not saying there is *anything* glamorous about Travelodges: there is a serious groundhog day feel after a couple of weeks staying in them.'

Their manager instilled the idea of breaking out of Ireland into the band, regularly booking them gigs in London, fully believing they had what it took to make it elsewhere. 'Dave gave us confidence as well,' says Pockets 'He had seen bands come and go before and stuff and he had us immediately going over to London for shows and people coming to see us. He taught us as well how much actual hard work it was, because he put us on these ludicrous tours that just wouldn't stop! So suddenly Mary and I were in the position that we had to drop out of college,' explains Pockets

'Which was rough for us, because we are both very close to our parents and both sets of parents would hold (as most parents do) a proper education in the highest regard. Everything they said, every argument we had with them made sense. Imagine your kid coming home saying, "I am leaving college to be a rock star," which wasn't exactly what we said but that's what they heard!' laughs MayKay.

'It sounded stupid, basically,' admits Pockets. 'I mean, there was absolutely no indication whatsoever that we were going to make a career of this when we left college. We just gave it up. There was no chance of us actually trying to do it, though, if we were still in college, because we wouldn't have been able to tour the way we did. It was a ludicrous decision to make but I am really glad I made it because we wouldn't be in the band if we'd stayed in college.'

Leaving college was not the only difficult thing MayKay had to face explaining to her parents. 'My parents would be very realistic and level-headed and trust me to make good decisions (most of the time),' laughs MayKay, 'but I wouldn't let them come to gigs. I had never considered what I was doing on stage to be in any way left-field but then as soon as they said, "Right, if you are going to leave college for this band we want to see the band you are leaving it for," I was just like, my dad *can't* come hear me say, "Did you fuck her, did you stick things up her," up on a stage, in front of five people!'

[Pockets attempts to suppress laughter as MayKay continues.]

'Maybe if you were playing to a thousand people it would be a different situation because you would think, "Oh well, maybe they get it." But to five people? I am leaving college to start threatening my ex-boyfriends? You know: murder! I couldn't let it happen. So that made life much harder for me because I made them stay away, while asking them for their full support in something that I wouldn't let them see.'

FLApes did the IMRO Tour in April 2007. Their first EP followed in May, put out on Irish indie label Fifa Records after Ashley Keating [the Frank and Walters] saw them play. Eventually MayKay's parents were invited to see them perform and it was for a landmark occasion; their first sold-out, headline show (proper) for the release of their second EP *David Carradine Is a Bounty Hunter Whos Robotic Arm Hates Your Crotch*. 'That is still one of my favourite nights ever,' says MayKay.

'That was great,' agrees Pockets.

'We were self-managed at that time also (management with Dave didn't work out: just contract things we couldn't figure out),' explains Pockets. 'We were more than willing to take on ten times as much work to do it ourselves. We would meet in the Library bar and go through lists of things we were going to do.'

'Keith Johnson [IMRO] and Angela Dorgan [FMC] were there to talk to if we needed advice or anything and they still are,' says MayKay

There was a serious buzz about the band within the industry and A&R from major labels started coming to the shows and talking about deals but nothing concrete had been offered. It was an Irish label that came up with what FLApes were looking for (Ashley Keating at Fifa Records understood that the band needed something bigger to help them progress).

'Niall Muckian [Director of Rubyworks and Model Citizen] came to a gig and said, "This is the deal I am offering." There was no bullshit about him. No: "I want to come see you again," or, "How many mailing list people do you have?" or, "How many MySpace friends do you have?" None of this crap, just, "I want to do your album. This is the idea I have: producer up to you; studio up to you; time limits up to you,"' recalls MayKay.

'It was just so on a plate,' says Pockets. 'Suddenly everything we wanted was on the table and it was a label we didn't know much about. All we knew was that they did Rodrigo y Gabriela and you know, that's very different to us. I think we said, "Here, this isn't really your thing," and I think his response was, "Do you think two instrumental Mexicans was my thing?" laughs Pockets.

'He made everyone so comfortable immediately, especially as we had just come out of being self-managed,' says MayKay.

Their début album, *Fight Like Apes and the Mystery of the Golden Medallion*, came out in September 2008 on the new alternative label Model Citizen, created by the people from Rubyworks: they were the first band to be released on it. It was recorded in Seattle with

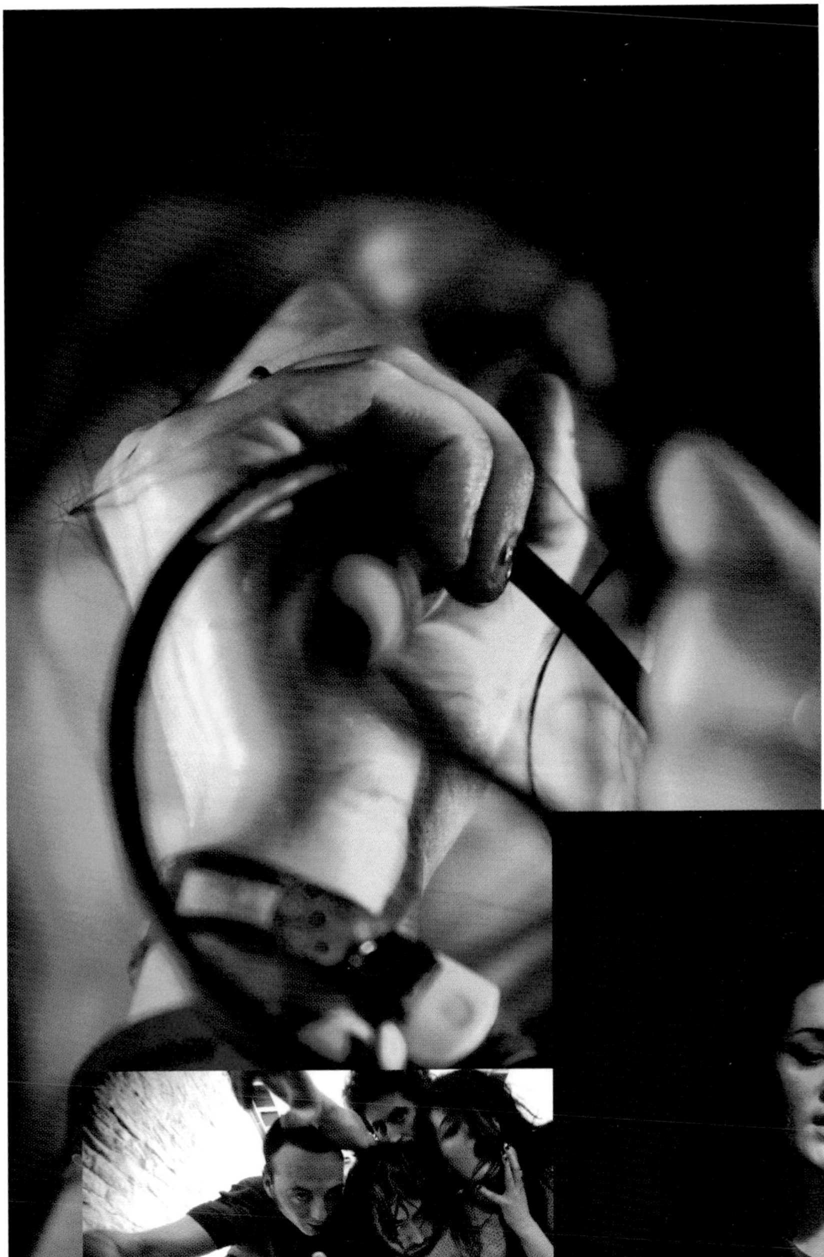

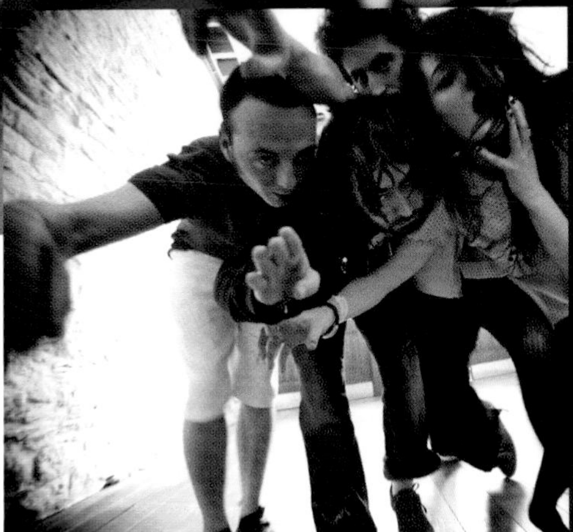

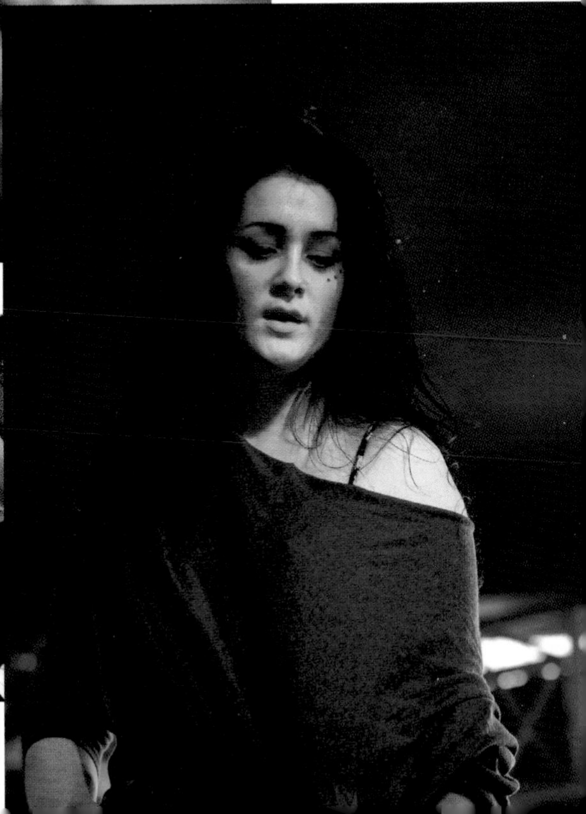

John Goodmanson. 'We planned to do the album really quickly once we decided on John but we were touring so much it was hard to get a full month to do it. It was ten or eleven months after the second EP that the album came out,' explains MayKay.

FLApes create strong reactions with their music. They like to be different, they push creative and industry boundaries: it's what makes them stand out. Their EP and album titles are long, with intentional misspellings (Whos), they take samples from B-movies and they write about things most bands don't (or wouldn't) write about. It results in two very clear opinion camps on the band: love and hate. They have had as much abuse in press and in blogs as they have had praise. 'We always knew we would be a band that you like or hate,' says Pockets 'We were surprised when we started to get so much positive press. We were waiting for a backlash... 'and then it came!' he laughs. 'We have ridiculously thick skin. People see us and think we are cocky brats, which we are, so it's OK – people can get really offended by us.'

MayKay smiles: 'Any extreme emotion is fine.'

FLApes have played New York and the legendary South by Southwest festival in the States. They find that they have to chat up a new audience to show that they have a sense of humour and that they are not really *that* excited about things like fish 'n' chips ['Canhead']. 'Apparently we are avant experimental,' reveals Pockets with a grin 'That was our publicity in SXSW. I think we are about as arty as a fucking diaper!' he says, laughing.

Things are going extraordinarily well for FLApes. In 2008 they landed a big booking agent in the UK, ITB, that they met when supporting the Von Bondies. Through them they have been given tour support with the Ting Tings and the Prodigy and played all the major UK festivals, including *The John Peel Show* at Glastonbury, Bestival, the Great Escape, Latitude, T in the Park in Scotland, Reading Festival and Leeds Festival. 'Their roster is insane,' says MayKay.

'We did the Von Bondies and then we toured the shit out of the UK on our own backs, then the Ting Tings and then Prodigy and now when we go back we are actually filling venues,' says Pockets. 'It's amazing to see what you can do in a year,' – if you work like crazy and lug your own gear like FLApes did.

'That was the amazingness that was 2008,' agrees MayKay.

2009 has followed suit. The album *Fight Like Apes and the Mystery of the Golden Medallion* has come out in the UK, Benelux, Australia and Japan. It was re-released in July as a festival edition with a bonus disc including rare tracks and B-sides. In September it was released in Germany, Austria and Switzerland on Strange Ways and this was followed by a series of live dates.

FLApes have also released a five-track EP on Model Citizen in North America, called *You Filled His Head with Fluffy Clouds and Jolly Ranchers. What Did You Think Was Going to Happen?*

Tours of Japan and Australia are next on the agenda for FLApes, which is something they are very excited about. The album came out in Japan on Sony Music in April 2009 and has been getting very good press. Sony had worked with their manager Niall on Rodrigo y Gabriela and when they heard FLApe's album they said they wanted it: 'I think they thought we were more pop than we were, (probably more like the Ting Tings) but we had already signed the contracts,' laughs MayKay. 'They said after the show that we were heavier than they thought but they loved that.' In Australia the album is out on Shock, one of the biggest indie labels there.

The band is also excited about everything that the USA and Canada have to offer (talks with labels are underway) but after touring Ireland and the UK for the last three years they are understandably a bit daunted by the size of North America. 'We are looking forward to the possibility of America but once you start you don't stop!' says Pockets.

As for recording album number two, they are looking forward to it. They just need some time off. 'Me and Mary will always write,' says Pockets. 'It's just a case of getting the four people together. We have been playing the same songs for two years, so I don't even know what it would sound like. Most of the songs were written in our first two weeks!'

'We need to get us some broken hearts in the next few months,' jokes MayKay. 'You start writing, I will go out with some dickhead and we will be fine!' she says, laughing.

The songs for the second album are well on their way with sneak previews during the summer festivals of new songs, 'Jenny Kelly' and 'Not a Merry Man' (the latter a quote from Warf during an episode of *Star Trek*).

As for the goal; it's all about having fun, travelling and exponential growth. 'I just want to be bigger again and bigger again,' says Pockets.

If the current trajectory of Fight Like Apes is anything to go by, getting bigger is a given. Their talent and their work ethic combined can only lead to extraordinary things.

Mick Flannery

Artist
Mick Flannery

Albums
Evening Train
White Lies

EPs
Mick Flannery

Label
EMI

Management
Lorcan Ennis, Verge Management

Websites
www.mickflannery.com
www.MySpace.com/mickflannery

Mick Flannery is intriguing. He's a down to earth, intelligent guy whose eyes talk when his lips don't. Mick may be shy but he is also extremely funny. He has a sharp, self-deprecating humour and a serious twinkle in his eye. He is a self-confessed mumbler, who early on in his career was known for singing to his shoes rather than to his audience.

Mick paints vivid pictures with his music. He draws you into stories with an amazing voice that sounds far older than its years. He has a dedicated and rapidly growing following, gathered through extensive radio play, television performances and constant touring.

He won first place in two categories of the USA Songwriting Competition in 2005 for songs from his début album, Evening Train. Mick's second album, the platinum-selling White Lies, was shortlisted for the Choice Music Prize Irish Album of the Year 2008 and he won a Meteor Award for Best Irish Male 2009. Mick has played virtually every venue in Ireland, including headline shows in the Marquee in Cork and Vicar Street in Dublin. He has also done a full UK tour supporting Kate Walsh and played numerous Irish festivals, including Sea Sessions and Electric Picnic.

'My mother's side is musical. All her brothers and sisters and her father used to sing all the time, not professionally, but they used to meet up at this bar called the Vintage in Killarney. It's gone now, which is a shame, but my uncle seemed to be a stalwart there, so they let us stay on afterwards and the guitar would come out and everybody would sing a song. They used to do Tracy Chapman and Tom Waits – all old cool stuff,' remembers Mick. 'I sang a lot with them but I was into Nirvana and stuff like that. I tried to sing a couple of Nirvana songs but it wouldn't really go over because they wouldn't know what I was on about. You'd hear, "What's he singing there?" but it was great craic.'

It was nights like this that inspired Mick to learn the guitar, watching others accompanying themselves as they sang. 'I thought that was cool,' he says. 'I was self-taught because I'm left-handed but we had a right-handed guitar at home. It was my mother's guitar and she didn't want me to switch the strings around; I just started learning with it upside down and then I just didn't go back to the proper way of playing. It makes it a small bit difficult if someone wants to jam along with me! I can tell what chords people are playing by the shapes but when I'm playing the shapes are different, so people can't really jam along with me that easily.'

Even so, Mick has no plans to get a left-handed guitar: 'I wouldn't bother learning how to play a left-handed guitar now; I just couldn't be arsed,' he laughs.

When Mick performs live, he splits his time between guitar and piano. 'I actually learned to play the piano first. I got sent to piano lessons when I was twelve or thirteen and I hated it. It was too uncool when you're thirteen. You'd miss soccer training because you were going to piano lessons – you would get such a kicking! You see, Mam and Dad wanted me to do something musical, so then when I took up the guitar I said, "Look, I'm playing the guitar. Can I give up the piano now?" and they said, "OK, grand."'

'The fella I had teaching me piano just taught you tunes, so when I learned guitar chords, I just transferred them on to the piano and started playing that way. It's a really basic way and I'm not a very good piano player but it was nice because I could learn Tom Waits songs then on the piano.'

Mick started experimenting with composing early on. 'I got an electric guitar when I was sixteen and I could plug it into my stereo system up in my room and play it through the small speakers: I'd no amp. It was really quiet and it was an old stereo but it was a decent thing that was just banged up a bit. Shit guitar, *really* shit guitar, but you could record what you were doing on to tapes so I was messing around. It was all crap. I still have all the tapes but it was brutal,' says Mick with a grin.

Mick's first foray into the recording process wasn't exactly successful. He was sixteen and his band decided to record one of his earliest compositions: 'It cost us about £150 to record it, which was really expensive, I thought, and we were brutal: it was horrible! That was the first time I ever played anything to anyone else and I stopped then for a while because I thought, "That's crap." It was just atrocious, an embarrassment. I remember listening back; I was definitely trying to be Kurt Cobain!'

This Cobain obsession carried through to his first public performance, covering two Nirvana songs at a session downstairs in the Lobby: 'Ricky Lynch and the Lynch Mob were playing, I loved them. They used to play every Monday night. I was under-age but my dad used to bring me in. Any song they'd play, I'd go up afterwards and ask, "Who's that?" and then I would go and buy the CD. They were brilliant and it was a thrill for me to be playing with them. I did 'The Man Who Sold The World' [MTV Unplugged in New York, David Bowie, 1970, and Nirvana, 1994] and 'Come As You Are' [Nevermind, 1992] and it was pretty bad too but I enjoyed it.'

Mick's natural shyness means that performing in public couldn't have been easy for him early on. 'I wasn't always comfortable. I got very nervous. I don't know why I put myself through it sometimes,' he admits. 'I asked myself before gigs, "What have I done to myself, what am I doing?" but you just get a kick out of it when it's over. I'm starting to relax a bit more, just let go a bit. I used to get very uptight. I think I've stopped staring at my shoes throughout the whole gig but it's baby steps for me!' laughs Mick.

After leaving school, Mick studied music at Coláiste Stiofán Naofa in Cork, where he learned about everything from sound engineering to music theory.

'I met a lot of good people in that course, a load of good musicians,' he says. 'I started playing in bands. The course put on gigs twice a year so you got to experience playing live. It was brilliant. The guitar player playing with me now and the violin player, I met them at the course and we've been playing pretty much ever since.'

As the college course took up only three days a week, Mick found himself practising stone-masonry for the rest of the week, a skill he learned during school breaks. Sightings of his van at gigs, bearing the legend, 'Mick Flannery, Stone Mason,' on the side, have been a source of mild bemusement to fellow musicians and added to his down-to-earth reputation.

Mick's début album, *Evening Train*, came about as a result of a project he set himself in his second year of college. 'I wanted to write more songs, I didn't have many songs really and I had one that was a kind of storyline thing, with two brothers in the story, and I said I'm going to develop this thing into a whole album. I didn't finish it in the year, I finished it about three months after I left. It was supposed to a musical first of all.'

Mick took some time to research musical theatre and read books on Gilbert and Sullivan and various other composers but he was never happy with the dialogue he wrote. He approached others to finish that side of it in college but it never really worked out to his satisfaction.

'I tried to write the dialogue and it was just awful, trite crap. I ended up writing a little narrative thing, that's clichéd enough as it is. If I'd had a finished product, maybe some theatre could possibly have put it on but I didn't have experience. A couple of fellas came to me saying, "Yeah, let's make a theatre thing of it," but it never really came to fruition,' says Mick.

He did perform it in full though: twice: 'I fuckin' mumbled the story in between songs and just told the thread but people can't understand what I'm saying half the time!' laughs Mick. 'I just did it nervously and awkwardly. I've given up on that now but it was an interesting idea.'

It may not have been fully staged or completed, but *Evening Train* showed the industry what a talent Mick was. He went to America for three months after college, at the age of twenty-one, and pressed the album there. While in the States, he entered the USA Songwriting Competition, a leading international competition with Tom Waits, Peter Hook and Loretta Lynn amongst the judges. Two of his songs became finalists in their categories from almost 15,000 entries ('The Tender' in Lyrics Only and 'In the Gutter' in Folk/Singer-Songwriter). Both won.

When he returned home, Mick started selling his album in bars around Cork. 'I used to have a jar behind the bar in three bars in Cork: the Corner House, the Lobby and Charlies. I could walk into the Corner House, all intentions of just taking the money and saving it, but I'd have to have one pint (you can't just walk in and take the money) and then they hand you the jar and there might be €15 or €30 in the jar and there might be some people there and then over three bars, twice or three times a week, you end up drinking thousands! I wasted so much money: great times – never again, though.'

Mick met his manager, Lorcan Ennis, through an introduction from the Lobby's Pat Conway. It wasn't long before his new management deal paid off, Mick signing a five-album deal with EMI Music Ireland and licensed *Evening Train* to them for re-release. 'They're nice people; it's just one house: small office, twenty people,' says Mick.

He began recording his second album in Dublin with a producer the label had brought in to record a few of his demos. 'I didn't think we really clicked that well; I wasn't too sure. I was still kind of naïve and I didn't know how important it was or how much it would have an effect on what was to come,' he admits, describing the initial recording sessions as 'very stressful'. A change of engineer, some re-recording and mastering eventually put any studio demons to rest, and

White Lies enjoyed a tremendous reception upon its release in September 2008. 'Tomorrow's Paper' received massive daytime radio play, as did 'Safety Rope', and the album was shortlisted for the Choice Music Prize 2008. Mick was voted Most Promising Irish Act in the 2009 *Hot Press* Reader's Poll and won Best Irish Male at the Meteor Awards 2009.

Mick is happy that people like his music but he is not quite sure how he feels about the awards and nominations. 'It is nice but I just don't know how to reconcile it in my head,' he admits. 'I don't know why, maybe it's the wrong kind of mentality to have but I always think: ignore it. Not to be clichéd but just try and write a couple of decent songs, will ya! You haven't done a tap or work in a couple of weeks!' Despite his incredible talent, one gets the feeling that verbal self-flagellation is common in Mick's internal dialogue.

As for the future or ambitions, Mick would like to play things quietly: 'I don't know what I want, I'm kind of just drifting along. I remember when I was about fifteen or sixteen seeing someone playing in the Opera House and saying, "Jesus I think I could do that," but after a while that kind of went away, I don't have it any more; I don't have any yearning.'

Mick doesn't want to be a star or play stadiums, at the moment anyway. 'We played the Cork Opera House and some big places before and we always kind of prefer the smaller ones, little bars and back rooms; somewhere in-between would be nice. Vicar Street is a good size, it's a *great* size. It's amazing that we got to fuckin' play Vicar Street. I like that place!'

'I would like to do more gigs, travel to America and England and stuff like that. I've no real concept of success though,' he admits. 'I just want the same thing normal people want really. I wouldn't mind a house in the country and a dog, a pick-up truck, a nice wife, maybe some kids.'

Mick is still adapting to the success he has had and he finds the positive attention a bit overwhelming at times, particularly when he's surrounded by well-wishers after gigs. 'If there's a lot of people I just get nervous and I want to run away. It's strange. When I'm forty I'll be kicking myself, saying, "Why didn't you just fuckin' relax and have a good time?"' laughs Mick.

One gets the feeling that Mick doesn't quite trust that music is his career yet – that things are only just starting for him. 'I'm afraid to believe it because six months from now, I could be looking for a stone-mason's job and not be able to get one,' he notes, displaying his total lack of arrogance.

One of Mick's other charming idiosyncracies is that he barely moves his mouth when he sings. His husky, gravelly voice seems to come from out of nowhere; it's been joked that he would make a great ventriloquist.

'I don't know what the fuck that's about,' grins Mick. 'I just always do it: maybe I didn't want anyone to notice it was me.'

Sometimes the audience help Mick out, singing along to his songs. It may throw him a little at first but never in a bad way: 'It's nice. It's really flattering, I just end up smiling my ass off when it happens.'

Another thing that clearly means a lot to Mick is the respect of his peers. 'I heard a story – I don't know if it's true or not now – but there's this guy who plays on a Monday night in Charlie's Bar where I normally go; Hank Wedel is his name and I really like what he does: he's a great performer,' says Mick. 'I heard that he was going to play one of my songs, or had played one of my songs, and it was a really cool feeling. *That's* fuckin' cool, that's so much better than any fuckin' gong.'

With the extensive touring Mick and his band have been doing, you'd think it'd be impossible for him to find the time to write his third album, yet he has it nearly finished. 'We have ten or eleven songs almost ready,' he says. 'I think we need a couple more upbeat ones anyway, because at the moment it's all very spacious. We need something with a bit of rhythm, keep the lads happy. But it's going all right.'

This time around, he's planning to do most of the recording without the aid of a recognised producer, 'Unless they're going to get us some fuckin genius like Ethan Johns or what's his face with the beard – Rick Rubin, he'd be all right! I'd settle for him,' laughs Mick. 'That would be cool because I wouldn't be the most original arrangements person: it's nice to have someone else's input, ideas: someone creative.'

Mick Flannery combined with Rick Rubin or Ethan Johns? Yes please.

Fred

Band Members
Joseph O'Leary
Jamie Hanrahan
Justin O'Mahony
Jamin O'Donovan
Carolyn Goodwin

Albums
Can't Stop I'm Being Timed
*Making Music So You Don't
        Have To*
Go God Go

EPs
The Fred EP

Label
RCM Music

Management
Sheena Keane,
        Blue Grace Music

Websites
www.fredtheband.com
www.MySpace.com/fredtheband

Fred have an amazing energy about them: a euphoric, creative, energy.

They are an exceptionally funny, lovely bunch of people and a wee bit mad. *Good* mad. They make the most uplifting, booty-shaking, happy, electro, indie pop around.

Fred were a slow burn in Ireland. They didn't get the attention they deserved early on but everything came together for them with their third album *Go God Go*. Suddenly Fred were receiving critical acclaim from all corners of the music press. They had daytime national radio play from RTÉ Radio 1, 2fm and Today FM. They were invited to play on *Tubridy Tonight* and they were nominated for the Hope for 2009 award at the Meteor Ireland Music Awards.

They have sold out shows from Whelans to the Cork Opera House and everywhere in-between and played Oxegen, Electric Picnic, Hard Working Class Heroes and Thomond Park. *Go God Go* has been released internationally: in Canada on the very cool new indie label Sparks Music, in the USA on UFO and in Japan on King Records. Fred's single, 'Skyscrapers', had the much-coveted honour of Single of the Week on Canadian iTunes.

Fred have a long convoluted history, with various new members added over the years and other members leaving. They started out as a Kerry band called Fred the Purple-Haired Ninja in 1998.

Joe explains: 'Jamie, our current guitarist, was in a band with three others who are no longer in the band. They were Emmett, Christie and Liam and they were called Fred the Purple-haired Ninja. Jamie went away: he didn't leave the band but he went travelling for a year. While Jamie was away Emmett recruited three Cork people for the band, because it had been a Kerry band until then – myself, Eibhilín and Justin. So we were a five-six piece then.'

INTERVIEW WITH JOSEPH (JOE) AND JAMIN

'Myself and Justin are still in the band, Eibhilín left only last September [2008] – she left after ten years. Then Jamin popped up in 2003 [adding Limerick to the mix],' says Joe.

People could be forgiven for thinking they were a collective or had an open-door policy but it wasn't like that. 'We weren't really hippies or anything; it wasn't like, "Oh yeah, come on in!" We were trying to find a sound that we liked and the only way we knew of doing that was to invite more people along who could play stuff!' says Joe. 'The lads couldn't get any gigs under the name Fred the Purple-Haired Ninja,' laughs Joe, 'So we shortened it to Fred and we got gigs after that.'

Most of the band were still teenagers and in college.

'Emmett was a real networker and he knew one of the Ents officers so we represented UCC in a sort of intervarsity thing and we won it. I think it was possibly our second or third gig,' remembers Joe. 'We went to Limerick and we were playing on the Guinness gig rig as it was called back then and we won the thing and we thought that was it, we thought we were *made*!' laughs Joe.

It may have taken many more years for Fred to hit the national spotlight but this was the hope all along.

'For me, I always wanted to make a living out of it,' says Joe. 'And of course, conquer the world – because that's what anyone who joins a band, if they're being honest, that's what they do it for – to get out there.'

'People go on about artistic merit and of course that's important but you want to get out and see the world and, if you can, make a living out of it. Sure, what better way could there be? I think maybe for some of the others it was a small bit more for the laugh,' reflects Joe. 'I always take things too seriously, I think. I've mellowed a small

bit over time, though. And we *were* having a laugh. Jesus, you think you're the bee's knees when you're young and in a band anyway,' says Joe.

'Our third gig was in Limerick and our fifth gig was in Galway; so in no time we were getting out there. In Dublin, I've noticed bands didn't have to leave Dublin for ages because there's so much going on, and it's only later on that they start getting out. Whereas when you're from Cork, you do one gig in Cork and that's it: you can't really do that again for another while, so you *have* to get out,' says Joe. 'I remember Eamon Dorans; that was one of our first Dublin gigs. We were supporting someone: that was cool.'

Fred were travelling and gigging but had yet to release anything, because they were slowly trying to create new material that involved the new members.

'There was a bunch of songs written when I came into the band, so we were playing them for a good bit and then with three more people, we really started messing round with stuff – because you have to get that satisfaction or else you'll join another band,' says Joe.

'Five creative people with egos!' says Jamin

'You come together for the right reasons, to make music and for your own personal satisfaction, but you have to do it with a group. None of us wanted to be solo artists,' says Joe.

'You want to be in a group, the magic that's in being in a band,' agrees Jamin.

'Traditionally, and even now, we're really tedious over songs,' confesses Joe. 'They sound like they should be written in five minutes but they take for ever, we're really slow, so therefore it took longer to come around to the idea of recording. I think it was two years down the line before we started recording. We came out with a four-tracker that we copied ourselves [*Fred EP*, 2000]. I think Jamie and his Mum and Dad were at the computer, burning them one by one and we got the stickers and everything. I remember 'Splodge' and 'The Parsnip Song' were on it – some dodgy songs!'

Unlike a lot of new bands, Fred had no difficulty getting headline gigs in Cork: 'There are no big bands there,' explains Jamin.

'When we started, the Sultans [Sultans of Ping FC] and the Franks [The Frank and Walters] had stopped and they had been the two big bands out of Cork,' continues Joe. 'So if anyone came along it was, "You're our boys now," so it was no problem getting headline gigs.

They headlined the Half Moon Club in 2001, on the back of that EP, playing to two hundred and fifty people. 'In Cork that was the big one to sell out at the time,' says Joe.

Fred released their début album *Can't Stop I'm Being Timed* themselves in 2002. They continued to play and grow their fan base, while holding down jobs.

Making Music So You Don't Have To, their second album, was also self-released in 2005. It had great local and alternative radio play but Fred were far from a mainstream name. 'We were poor and unhappy,' says Joe.

'We're still poor!' reminds Jamin.

'Yeah, it's not all roses yet,' admits Joe.

'We used to get buses and Eibhilín would bring the whole back line in her Toyota Starlet. Now in fairness, we didn't have a very big back line and we still don't, but the drum kit; guitars and a couple of amps – *all* into her car. She would drive it up and her car would overheat, so when she hit traffic in Dublin she was sweating. It was nuts! The rest of us were getting buses that took

around six hours at the time but now we have a fancy broken-down van. A Ford Transit; it can fit about seven,' grins Joe

Behind the humour and great pop singles is a hard-working band. Fred rehearse every Tuesday and spend ages writing.

'There was, for a long while, too much of a sense of humour with Fred and people said, "Oh yeah, they're the funny guys, or they're the nice lads." We got an awful lot of that from the promoters and media and stuff. I wouldn't say we lost our sense of humour but we thought that if *we* didn't take it a bit more seriously how the hell would any one else take it more seriously? I suppose in the last three years we've held that attitude,' says Joe

Fred met their manager a few years ago at the Roundstone Arts Festival in Connemara. She has been a big part of the turnaround in the band and their success. 'We played one festival for her and then we went back the next year and played another one. Eventually she came to New York and planned a few gigs for us,' says Jamin.

'We cajoled her into it,' says Joe. 'Before she knew it she was our manager. It actually took a year and a half to two years, because at the time the boom was going on, so why the hell would you get involved with a band? I mean: bands don't make money, not the first couple of years anyway (if ever!). It's the hardest thing to find – a good manager in Ireland. It's easier to get a record deal. I think it took a year and a half of ringing her, asking her questions, getting help. Bit by bit she got more involved and then it came to the crunch and she kind of said, "Lads, what am I doing here? Am I your manager or what?" and we said, "Yeah, that was the plan," laughs Joe.

'It was kind of like a couple going out and they didn't know if they were boyfriend and girlfriend or not. For about a year!' laughs Jamin.

'Basically it took us ten years to learn,' says Joe. 'We were looking for management for a while and when she came on board we kind of sharpened up our act. She *forced* us to sharpen up our act. She shopped around for PR and we ended up with the girls and that's worked out great.'

Fred hired Lindsey Holmes Publicity (LHP) to promote their third album *Go God Go*. It was the first time they had paid for a full campaign to support an album and it worked wonders for the band's profile outside Cork. Some of the PR people Fred had spoken to during their search had been hesitant about the band: they were not sure how to market them. 'There's no particular genre you could put it in. We tick all the boxes! You could put two of the songs on the album together and you'd think they were different bands almost, bar the players. LHP took that as a really strong point.'

Fred are an alternative band, most often described by journalists as indie pop. 'We're really proud of the "pop" word. Jamie had problems handling it for a while but now that we're getting radio play he likes the word "pop"!' laughs Joe

'That was a bit of an issue for us a few years ago because we were too poppy to get played on the night-time shows and not poppy enough for the day time shows and we were like, "Where the fuck do we fit in?" because we did want to get played,' says Jamin

'Tony Fenton made 'Skyscrapers' the download of the day and you could see from that point on that there were little trends happening. For us, Tony Fenton is a cool motherfucker! Rick O'Shea has supported us and Dan Hegarty has been playing stuff for four or five years. It's mad: as soon as you get any bit of consistent play people start wondering if they're missing something. People started getting behind us more then. It was cool suddenly to start getting a bit of support. We can't really give out about the radio any more!' says Joe

'It's very encouraging. We have been full steam ahead now for the last year,' says Jamin.

Fred became the first band to play in the renovated Thomond Park stadium in Limerick. It was a huge honour for them. They played three singles, 'Running', 'Skyscrapers' and 'Good One', before Munster's Heineken Cup quarter-final match against the Ospreys (2009).

They can't believe the difference it made to them having an organised PR campaign and are annoyed with themselves that they hadn't factored one in properly before. 'The second album was recorded in the studio and we spent loads of money on it,' says Jamin.

'No budget for PR,' confesses Joe. 'We had no clue, to be honest. We were saying, "Ah, we should do something."'

'We had distribution for three months or something,' says Jamin.

Fred changed the approach completely for *Go God Go*. They recorded it themselves in a bedroom and a garden shed. 'The last album, we spent nothing on it. I don't know, a grand? We bought a computer but we got it mixed professionally [by Mark Wallis in London]. We wanted it to sound good enough for radio (to get the radio sound you need the outside mix) and we just got a good PR company, which worked out great.'

Being DIY is something Fred are very proud of. 'It costs nothing and you own it yourself,' says Jamin.

'We came to the stage where we didn't want to be the big fish in Ireland only and we're nowhere near being a big fish in Ireland – don't get me wrong – but even if you *got* that far, you'd want to get out,' says Joe.

Fred started work towards that goal by playing one of the big music industry festivals in the States: CMJ. 'It was cool to be in New York for the first time as a band. We went back once more. Not much happened but there was a bit of interest.'

Things went differently however, when they went to Canada. Fred played the North by Northeast Music and Film Festival (NXNE) in Toronto in July 2008. The interest was immediate.

One of the interested people was Jeff Rogers, one of the most widely respected artists and managers in the Canadian music industry, who has managed the Crash Test Dummies and been Head of Artist Development at Richard Branson's V2 label in New York. 'He and his buddies had set up this label called Sparks Music – they were all old heads from the business. He came along, couldn't see us, got really interested in the album, heard the album, got even more interested, played it for his buddies. They said, "Can we sign you up, can we distribute for you and be your record label in Canada?" It was like "OK!"'

Fred's album *Go God Go* was released in Canada on Sparks/EMI Music on 10 March 2009. It was preceded by the single and video for 'The Lights'.

'It happened really fast,' says Jamin. 'We have got lots of press and reviews, so we're kind of waiting to see how that goes. We did play a load of gigs over there.'

'We were on Canada AM [a hugely popular breakfast television news show]. It was cool. The label had set up a good bit: they sent stuff into iTunes from all their bands and they picked 'Skyscrapers' as the free download for the week. It was like 30,000 downloads! It was huge exposure for us and there were Canadian dudes actually making videos for it, just having the craic. It was crazy to see that this kind of stuff can happen,' says Joe.

'Skyscrapers' was the second single to be released in Canada (July 2009) and enjoyed radio play both by commercial and college radio. Legendary Canadian radio and TV presenter Alan Cross interviewed them on *Explore Music*. More TV and festival appearances followed for

Fred, including the famous Hillside Festival at Guelph Lake in Ontario.

Fred have toured the east of Canada and the Atlantic provinces extensively and have played Pop Montreal, Toronto Indie Week and Canadian Music Week (CMW). Things went so well for them in North America that their manager, Sheena, even relocated there for the summer.

Go God Go was released in the United States on United For Opportunity (UFO) Music on 26 May 2009. It was also released in Japan on King Records.

Many people in the music industry in Ireland feel that Fred have not had the media attention that they deserved over the years. One wonders if it is because they are not based in the capital with the national press and the major promoters?

'We haven't spent a lot of time in Dublin: we've spent a lot of time everywhere *but* Dublin,' admits Jamin. 'Maybe every three or four months we play a gig. We're away from the Dublin scene. The media is there, everything is there; that's the truth of it. It's the same in England, it's the same in Canada; any time we go [to Canada], we go to Toronto. Any time we go to England, we go to London.'

'We're out in Cork and we'll know anyone in Cork. Dublin is bigger. If you're out in Dublin (it's famous the Whelans crowd), you're hanging out with the journalists, the DJs, everyone. You're bound to make friends with a few of them! We have that down in Cork but really there's no national media down in Cork,' says Joe

It can be hard to keep a band together at the best of times and it gets even harder when finances are stretched. But Fred remain committed.

'We're all hopeless maybe four days a week and the other three we keep it going,' jokes Jamin. 'We haven't made it yet,' he says by way of an explanation. 'I guess we all want to do it really.'

'How we finance the band is that any money made from gigs and from records goes straight back into it. We take out nothing. It covers our expenses,' explains Joe. 'That's why we made the album ourselves. We do per diems when we tour but outside that, everything goes back in: PR, mixing, PR again. Our van keeps breaking down. We're working on giving ourselves something but we're nowhere near it! It'd be nice to buy an ice-cream for yourself and go, "Hey, I earned this," says Joe.

'We're still really poor,' says Jamin. 'Even my mother is asking me where the money is!'

'It's a massive frustration because if you didn't have to do all those little things on the side you'd have much more time to write your next album. That's why the last one took so long, because that's the only way we had of doing it,' says Joe.

With any luck, financial struggle is a thing of the past for Fred. With the overwhelmingly positive response they have had in North America, things have taken a dramatic turn for the good.

After the success of *Go God Go,* Fred are now focused on recording their next album. Most of the tracks are demoed and they hope to release it by summer 2010.

'We're fairly collaborative. Every song is different. Basically, people come in with ideas and sometimes those ideas could get worked on straight away and finished maybe within a month but more than likely they'll take two years to finish!' laughs Joe. 'Jamie would come in with stuff almost done and we'd say, "Can we strip it back a bit and add in our bit?"'

'It's better if you have space to clear your head and then come back with a few ideas. "The Lights" was written in bits and pieces. There was a riff and I messed around with it for a while and then Justin wrote some lyrics and we all wrote some lyrics. We're not like, "He's the songwriter." We're not that type of band,' says Joe

Fred returned to Ireland to play Oxegen 2009 and to do a national tour in November. A tour of America is planned for early 2010, which will be followed by their fourth album. Things couldn't be going any better.

Lisa Hannigan

Artist
Lisa Hannigan

Band
Tom Osander
Shane Fitzsimons
Donagh Molloy
Gavin Glass

Album
Sea Sew

Label
Hoop Recordings

Management
Bernadette Barrett

Websites
www.lisahannigan.ie
www.MySpace.com/lisahannigan

Lisa Hannigan is a tonic: you feel better for having spent time with her. She is luminous, one of those people who glows and radiates positivity, so it is no surprise that her début album turned out to be a joyful one.

Sea Sew is her platinum-selling début, which was shortlisted for the Choice Music Prize Irish Album of the Year, and Best Irish Album at the Meteor Awards, while Lisa herself was up for the Best Irish Female award. Perhaps more importantly, *Sea Sew* was then shortlisted for the very prestigious Mercury Prize album of the year [UK or Ireland]. Lisa and her band have performed on Jools Holland, *The Jay Leno Show*, *The Colbert Report* and Mercury Prize 2009 programmes and they've played numerous festivals from Glastonbury and Electric Picnic to Le Chéile and Cork X Southwest.

It's probably no surprise that Lisa ended up singing. She grew up in the country, in a house that loved music.

'We didn't sit around and play songs for each other by any stretch of the imagination but my parents were both into music – luckily! My mom is really into Joni Mitchell and Nina Simone, my dad was really into BB King, Christy Moore – more that kind of end,' says Lisa. 'There was a lot of music around and I think my first musical memory was sitting in the back of the car, singing along to 'Ladies of the Canyon' [Joni Mitchell,1970]. My mum would be singing the Joni Mitchell bit, my brother and me in the back going, "Bah, doo, doo doo." I must have been in a car seat because I remember the angle; the lean-back, so I must have been pretty young!'

Lisa used to sit in the car and play her tapes so that her brother wouldn't bother her, a memory that makes her laugh. 'I remember getting into Michael Jackson: I was *so* into Michael Jackson and *Bad* was my first tape. My friend and I used to come up with dance routines for the *whole* record. From there, I got *Off the Wall* and *Thriller*. We couldn't dance like Michael Jackson; we would do our own routines,' laughs Lisa. 'So obsessed!

'I was always into music and then when I went to primary school, my best friend's mum was a guitar teacher so I did a bit of classical guitar. I used to go over to her house and her mum taught us music theory and stuff and we were only tots – we were only seven or eight really. I did that for a few years and that is why, to this day, I still cannot strum the guitar to save my life! I find it really hard to strum in time – I have no rhythm at all! I have my own little rhythm for singing, which is fine, but if I am playing guitar, everyone else is like, "Stay in time with the drums!" But still, I can only pick the guitar really.'

Lisa also remembers recorder classes from school: thirty children playing 'Mary Had A Little Lamb'. 'I was quite into the recorder,' confesses Lisa. 'I liked it. That's all we did; danced to Michael Jackson and the recorder!'

Eventually Lisa moved on to Nirvana and Kristin Hersh, learning some of their songs on guitar. She had heard 'Your Ghost', Hersh's duet with REM's Michael Stipe [*Hips and Makers*,1994] on the radio and tracked down the record, something much more difficult to do before the internet, especially when you live in a very small town without a record shop.

'I listened to *Hips and Makers* solidly and it is still one of my favourite records. I went to see [Hersh] in the Temple Bar Music Centre back when I was sixteen or something and she was absolutely incredible. I remember that was the first time I had gone into town by myself and sought her out. She did an in-store the next day in Tower. I queued up and probably asked really stupid questions!'

There was no question in Lisa's mind as to what she wanted to be: 'I definitely wanted to be a singer. For a while, I wanted to be an opera singer. My mum brought me home a compilation of arias; it was all the hits and there was this one song with all these different sopranos singing. It was "The Bell Song" from *Lakme* and even for me now, just technically; it's crazy. As a kid, just thinking it was the coolest thing I had ever heard and I got into Maria Callas and just listened to Maria Callas for a year or two. That's all I wanted to do: to be an opera singer.'

It was the fact that opera was so difficult, so technical, that attracted Lisa: 'It was such an art. That one hundred per cent of your life had to be about that, I just found that really attractive and her voice really effective. I was mad into it for years and then I just realised I'm not an opera singer at all, what am I thinking?'

Lisa got involved in singing competitions as a teenager, something a lot of people in her school were doing: 'There was a group of us really into singing and we'd do all the feises and stuff. That was my thing. I was always into singing. I was never in the school musicals or anything because I had a really tiny, tiny voice, really quiet; so I never got any parts. I remember when the list was put on the notice board, there was a lot of tears, a lot of tears specifically from me!' laughs Lisa. 'It was only when I got a microphone and I met Damien that it was like, sweet! And then through having the microphone, I got louder; through confidence, probably.'

After school Lisa moved to Dublin and went to Trinity College, which is where she met Damien Rice. 'I did French and Art History in Trinity for a couple of years. I just wanted to go to college and meet people and be in the Theatre Club and see all the great stuff and go to gigs and live in town, because I'd always lived in the country.'

Lisa grew up in Kilcoon, County Meath: 'It was pretty full-on country, so when I came to college it was definitely a big change. It was a great change. It was really exciting to be in Trinity and go to gigs and be around town. Everything was just there. I had worked really hard in school and then I went to college and I think I went to the library twice, one of which was the library tour! I just spent a lot of time smoking rollies and drinking coffee and reading my philosophy book – reading my Sartre,' laughs Lisa. 'Check me out!'

'I met Damien the first day of college, the first day of Fresher's Week,' recalls Lisa. 'I bumped into him in a pub on Westmoreland Street and chatted very briefly. I just kept meeting him around town and I didn't know anything about him. He was in a band I had never heard of before and wasn't into and at some point he said, "Hey, I need a girl to sing on this one particular song." And I went over to his house in Celbridge, which was very close to where I was from. I used to go over to his house and sing, I didn't know how to record or anything, it was all really amazing; really good craic. I started singing more and more songs and he would give me more and more bits to do and guitar lines here and there and we just started working all the time.'

She remembers their first gig, in Whelans: 'It was probably a month or something after we started singing, so that was quite nerve-racking. I was wearing a denim skirt, with a belt for putting my thumbs in, and just kind of standing there trying to look relaxed. I sang and it was the most nerve-racking experience ever. I remember the awkward way I held [the microphone], like being on a first date: look relaxed!'

Lisa was in college while they were recording Damien's album O but eventually she gave up college. 'I left after two years. It was just too much.' Describing the recording process as 'the best craic ever', Hannigan also confesses that they 'worked our holes off' during the two-year process.

To most people it seems like Damien was an overnight success but Lisa says there was a lot of time that passed before there was any real momentum. 'There was so long doing the rounds. We did a few tours with the Frames around Ireland, which was amazing; it was at just the right point.'

What followed was years of American and international touring, success and critical acclaim. As Damien's backing singer, Lisa witnessed it all: the tours, the TV shows, the festivals, the attention. She was part of it all but not centre-stage. Both fans and media always felt it was just a matter of time until Lisa went off on her own and was offered a big solo deal but that didn't happen – at least not when or how people expected it to.

'People did see me as Damien's backing singer, which I was. I was singing somebody else's music,' admits Lisa. 'I turned a couple of things down but they weren't real offers or anything.

'I wanted to do it by myself and I knew I wanted to write my own songs – I kind of deflected anything that didn't feel right. I was pretty young and I was just gathering my songs. I think working with Damien, being friends with Damien, knowing other people like Paul Noonan and Glen Hansard – I found that quite intimidating as a songwriter. You would see people literally lash out an amazing song in ten minutes and I could barely play the guitar, couldn't play the piano. I thought of myself more as a singer than a songwriter and didn't have that much confidence in songwriting. So it took me a while actually to think: maybe I *can* write songs, as opposed to just being a singer. I had myself in that area, even though I had written songs, just standing next to these towering songwriters.'

Lisa first started writing songs while touring with Damien; on the bus itself. 'I would have notebooks and have bits of lines here and there. I had an awful lot of first line, first curses; where you start a song, "Doo, doo, doo,' and then get a first verse and then don't know what to do. Because I'm not the best guitar player, I find it hard to frame a song, I've got better but at the time that was my trouble. So I just had verses here and there, lines written and melodies and the bass line and all these jumbled kinds of stuff, all gathered.'

Lisa had found confidence in her writing but was so busy touring with Damien that she never had the time that she needed to put it all together.

Her six-year musical partnership with Damien Rice ended in March 2007. 'Once that was over, I just threw myself into it and finished writing all the songs and arranging them and gathering the band.'

Today she works with many of the musicians who played with Damien Rice. 'I knew I was always going to work with Tom Osander [and the rest] because they were my friends. Whenever I had a song on tour, I would always be like, "Here, let's have a mess at this." And with the lads, if I had a bass line, I'd be like, "Shane, do you mind playing that? I just want to work out a thing on top," so they were always involved. It was pretty natural when everything moved together.'

Lisa arranged the songs with her friend, London-based engineer Jason Boshoff, as the rest of the band were still working with Damien. By the time they were free to join her, the album was ready to record: 'I'm a big list-maker and I'd planned out the artwork and a group of songs that we would choose from and it was very natural in the way it all happened. I'd planned it as far as I could and then gathered the band and rehearsed. We went down to Tomo's house and rehearsed for a couple of months in the barn. Amazing craic!'

Sea Sew came out on Lisa's own label, Hoop Recordings, on 12 September, 2008. The artwork for the album was done in-house, all hand-stitched by Lisa with the help of her mother, Frances. Having heard Lisa sing only other people's songs (with Damien, *The Cake Sale* album and various charity nights) people did not know what to expect; *Sea Sew* came as a surprise.

'People definitely didn't expect it to be cheerful!' laughs Lisa. 'I found that out from people: "I thought it was going to be a bit more kind of haggard as a vibe,"' imitates Lisa, laughing. 'I supposed Damien's vibe is a bit more kind of down. I was having so much craic as well, the record ended up being kind of cheerful.'

Lisa was now fully in the spotlight and the pressure and expectation were centred on her. 'I definitely gained a lot of perspective,' she admits. 'God, the pressure he [Damien] must have been under, because I didn't realise till it was me how it is and how it's not just the songs or the music, it's the general vibe of a gig that is your responsibility. It's the atmosphere, the stuff that you think you don't have any control over. It is your responsibility when you are the front person and I totally didn't realise that till I was there and that was the tough bit. Somebody breaks a string; somebody has to say something, make a joke or sing a song or whatever it is: you have to do it. That was the stressful bit. For ages I was just like, "Lads, somebody say something, make a joke!" Now I'm good. Finally.'

As a backing singer, Lisa did not talk to the audience. 'I never would have spoken into a microphone. I never would have spoken between songs and that was the weird bit. It is nerve-racking. Singing is so natural to me but speaking, making jokes, that's not the most natural!' laughs Lisa. 'I don't think I would have been able to get up with my guitar by myself and just do it. To have them there [the band, her friends] is so much easier, so much fun.'

Sea Sew was a critical hit, with the singles 'Lille' and 'I Don't Know' getting extensive radio play in Ireland and the UK. Awards and nominations soon followed with the *Hot Press* readers' poll, the Choice Music Prize and the Meteor Awards. Then in July 2009 Lisa was nominated for the Mercury Prize, the very prestigious UK and Ireland music award. She is among a very select list of Irish artist to have made the shortlist over the years, an incredible boost to her profile and a huge critical pat on the back.

Technically Lisa is a singer-songwriter but as with many of her contemporaries, it's not a label that feels right. 'I definitely associate singer-songwriters with someone singing with their guitar about their feelings,' she admits. 'So much emphasis for me is on arranging the songs interestingly, as opposed to me playing on the guitar and everybody playing along. There's something about the term that I turn away from. And there's a slightly sad vibe about it as well, which I'm not into. I've loved so much singer-songwriter music in my time but I feel a bit more cheerful now,' laughs Lisa. 'And you know, you can't have a trumpet when you're a singer-songwriter!'

Trumpet isn't the only upbeat, non-standard instrument in Lisa's musical repertoire: she has glockenspiel, bells, shakers and harmonium. 'I've tried to use interesting instruments,' she says. 'I don't want the standard thing. First of all, because I can't play guitar. With the harmonium you pump with one hand and play with this hand, so it just suits me perfectly. I can hide my shyness!' says Lisa

Lisa did a lot of really small gigs to get used to being in the middle of the stage, including tours of Cork, Kerry and Kilkenny. 'I was so excited after all the gigs. I definitely started to lose that kind of nervous excitement during the years with Damien and it just felt completely new again, like I had never sung before for people, so nerve-racking and exciting. We toured so much. It was just great and by the end of it, I felt able for it and then we got this offer for this American support tour, out of the blue.'

That support was a huge North American tour with Jason Mraz: 'It was more gigs than we'd ever done together as a band. Huge venues. When the offer came in, I got the list of these dates and it was like Radio City Music Hall, Ryman in Nashville, Massy Hall in Toronto. Dream venues that I had never played and I was just, "Oh God, what are we going to do? We are digging the hugest most unfathomable hole for ourselves [financially] but we had to make it happen. So we went.'

'We lived on the bus. Normally people travel on the bus and stay in hotels on days off but we just lived on the bus and showered at the venues and it wasn't luxury but we did our best. We saved money everywhere we could and tried to sell as many CDs and T-shirts as we possibly could, pimped ourselves out at the merch stand as much as possible,' laughs Lisa. 'We met this American record company, ATO Records, when we were there and they said they wanted to put the record out in North America, so we licensed it to them [released January 2009].

'It was just brilliant, I've never had so much craic. We played for forty minutes a night; for a support? They gave us such an opportunity to play and it was such a nice audience; people sat and listened. It was just crazy!' says Lisa

Some amazing opportunities have come Lisa's way and the best one was by pure chance. American television host Stephen Colbert invited her to perform on his show *The Colbert Report*, a very rare invitation, as the show does not typically feature music: 'That came about because we made some videos with Donal Dineen down in Kerry.'

Lisa had a couple of gigs in Dingle, so they rented a house for a week and took advantage of the time they had there and the wonderful character of the local pubs. 'I thought it would be good to make some videos while we were down there, so I asked Donal and some friends to come down and we'd maybe make a video for 'Lille' but maybe we'd just film loads of videos of us in pubs – you know, do some tunes. We ended up getting loads of videos and put them on the internet. Stephen Colbert was viewing Sean Hannity and this thing popped up and he was just watching it. He had

his headphones on while his wife was asleep, and thought these videos were really cool and flicked around loads of them, called his producer the next day and said, "Who are these people? Let's have them on the show." When we first got the call, we thought it was amazing and that it was a record company thing but now I know it was actually him flicking around on YouTube. He doesn't have music on the show: I think he had only David Byrne and Wilco,' says Lisa in disbelief. 'Mad!'

Lisa and the band performed 'I Don't Know' on the show and performed 'Lille' for the audience afterwards: 'That was one of my favourite days of life, *ever*, and all the lads were the same. It went really well.'

Having already toured North America, been nominated for a Mercury Prize and performed on famous TV shows, Lisa is living her dream. So one wonders is there is anything that she is itching to achieve?

'I just want to get better. Better in terms of songwriting and singing and poster-making and video-making and everything. There are so many aspects to it that are fun and you have such an opportunity to make everything yourself. I'd like to get better as a musician because I'm a bit shit at playing instruments: I've always thought of myself as a singer. I'd love to be better at that and to play gigs with my friends. That's all I want; to play more and more interesting gigs and for us to be more creative onstage and just get better. Really, there's nothing more that I want.

'I certainly wouldn't measure any ambitions in terms of numbers. To have more of those days where you go to sleep going, "*That* was amazing, I can't believe I got to do that!" The more of those days you can rack up, the better!'

Lisa has already begun work on her second album, despite the hectic schedule she has had since the release of *Sea Sew*. 'I have a few songs written. I haven't really had time. I've got a week now where I can hopefully write a song or two but I don't know what direction it's going to go. I have to see how the songs come out.

'I would quite like to have a record that you would put on when you are getting ready to go out; a little bit more exciting or funky or one that makes you excited about going out. But I don't know. We will see! I have that idea in my head that I would like to do that eventually,' says Lisa. 'Don't hold me to it. I'll probably do some terrible, miserable record!'

Impossible.

Jape

Artist
Richard Egan (Richie)

Albums
Cosmospher

The Monkeys in the Zoo Have
  More Fun than Me

Ritual

Label
V2/Cooperative Music

Management
Phil Morais, CEC Management

Websites
www.MySpace.com/richiejape

Richie is a bundle of enthusiasm and positive energy. He is a bit of an electro-pop genius with folk melody influences and laid-back charm. He strikes you as a musician who is in it for life, constantly experimenting and creating innovative sounds. He is well-liked and respected in the industry and fellow musicians have turned to him for mixes of their singles, including the somewhat legendary Jape remix of Fight Like Apes's 'Battlestations'.

The single 'Floating' from Jape's second album, *The Monkeys in the Zoo Have More Fun than Me,* started as an alternative radio hit and then became a sensation when the Raconteurs started to perform it in their sets. Richie's growing fan base and profile were given another dramatic boost when Jape won the Choice Music Prize Album of the Year 2008 for *Ritual*. He was nominated for Best Irish Male at the Meteor Ireland Music Awards the same year. He has played numerous Irish, UK and European festivals, including Glastonbury, Bestival and Electric Picnic.

Before Jape came to public attention, Richie Egan was known to music fans as the bass player in the Dublin instrumental band, the Redneck Manifesto. The band met and formed through a mutual love of American punk. 'I started going to Hope Collective gigs back in the early 1990s: we started going to all those DIY punk gigs. I was in a band called Black Belt Jones; I used to play bass and sing in that band and then through those gigs met up with all the other members of Redneck Manifesto, who were all in different bands. We just started to jam together instrumentally and we came up with the Rednecks. We did our first gig in 1998, I think.'

On the side Richie was writing and playing at home but in a very different style and genre. 'I was always interested in more melodic stuff like Simon and Garfunkel and Beck and stuff like that.' The sort of sounds you wouldn't hear in the

Redneck Manifesto. 'That was an outlet that I wanted,' explains Richie. 'I used to record songs in the house on a four-track, ever since I was a kid: I ended up with a lot of songs so my friends were saying, "Maybe you should do a gig."'

'I started off under my own name: Richard Egan. After a while I made an album, basically a really small album, in a house in the country with an Adat machine. Leagues and David O'Grady from Volta wanted to put it out but I didn't want to use my own name for a recorded thing because it felt more official, I wanted it to be a little bit more ambiguous.'

Cosmosphere came out on Volta Sounds in 2003. It was a small run – only 500 copies. 'That was my first time to use the name Jape,' says Richie. 'I can't remember where I got the name, I think one of my friends may have given it to me. I actually don't like the name,' admits Richie. 'Someone said to me that it kinda sounds like a toilet cleaner and I'd have to agree with that,' he laughs

'I think it has something to do with an ape, it would've been Richard Ape but that would have been Rape so we wouldn't have been able to call a band that, so Jonathan Ape is what we came up with or something, some weird stupid story. Anyway, that's where Jape came from! I just stuck it down because I wanted to have the live band be a little unpredictable, so that people didn't know what they were going to get when they came to see it and I still actually like that idea of it.' Jape is more of a musical entity than a person. 'I always think of Jape as the band; I don't think of it as myself.'

'I remember reading an interview with Nick Cave, and when you're playing with musicians live you can't really tell them what to do because it stifles them a lot, I think. So you just give them the songs, the basic working material, and they can do what they like over it and often times they'll come up with stuff that's really good and really

surprising to you.

All the people I play with, there's kind of like a revolving door but I trust them all so much musically, they wouldn't play anything crap, ever!' laughs Richie. 'You just have to find the people you gel with musically.'

Richie has not left the Redneck Manifesto and has no intention of doing so: 'I'm still part of the Rednecks,' he explains. 'The good thing about Jape and the Rednecks is that they're completely different, it's like doing Maths and writing an English essay: it's a different part of the brain,' says Richie. 'With the Rednecks, we only ever write together in a room and the five of us are there but outside that room we don't write for the Rednecks: the only stuff I do is for Jape. So the Rednecks is very much a group, hive-mind thing we just do together. It's completely democratic.'

The Redneck Manifesto recorded a new album with Dave Odlum, in Black Box studios in France, in June 2009, just before Richie started work on recording his fourth album for Jape. They are really happy with the results.

Richie says that the Rednecks continue because it's so enjoyable and they know that they are good, rather than because they hope to get somewhere with it. 'We have a very good relationship; we're like a gang, we'll never break up because we're too close. We're like family and we don't really have any ambition apart from just jamming together; so that's fairly easy to keep going. We'll keep going until we die – one of us dies!' laughs Richie.

It's a different vibe with Jape, though: 'Maybe I've always had slightly more ambition than some of the other lads in the band, in the sense that I'd like to make my career from music. With the Rednecks we just can't do that for a few reasons, logistical reasons, so with Jape I decided to give it a shot and take it a little more seriously.'

A few years ago Richie packed in his job to concentrate on music full-time and avoid regret in later life. 'Even to know that you tried your best and you failed rather than just sitting there going, "Maybe, maybe if I had tried..." So I just said, "Fuck it, I'll give it my best shot."

His second album, *The Monkeys in the Zoo Have More Fun than Me,* came out on the Dublin Indie label Trust Me I'm a Thief in September 2004.

Jape had a good following at that stage, (the first headline show took place just before the release of *The Monkeys in the Zoo*) but it wasn't until he started working on material for *Ritual* that he felt things really start to click. 'It takes me a while to get my head around things,' confesses Richie. 'With Jape I spent a lot of time doing stupid things like playing gigs with a Gameboy and stuff like that, basically just messing.' Over time he realised that he really enjoyed the gigging side of Jape, so he felt he should take it more seriously.

'The one where I felt, "*Now* I've really got it!" was supporting the Russian Futurists in Whelans. I had worked hard on the set, they were all new *Ritual* songs but I knew the songs were good; and I knew the band was tighter and we fuckin' rocked the place that night. That was like, "Right, this is cool, I'm going in the right direction with this!"'

Without knowing it, Jape was about to be catapulted into the spotlight. Singer Brendan Benson had heard Jape's single 'Floating' when he was in Ireland and asked the DJ who it was. When he came back next it was with his band with Jack White, the Raconteurs. Loving the song, they decided to cover it in their set at the Olympia, crediting Jape on stage on the night (Brendan rang him beforehand to tell him they were going to play it, so Richie was there.) They also played it in the UK and at various shows on the tour.

'Yeah, that was kinda cool,' agrees Richie 'But "Floating" was out two or three years when that happened. It was good in the sense that I had my demo CD with the *Ritual* songs on it and people came knocking, looking to hear shit and I was able to give them ten songs straight away (that I considered to be really good), so that was cool. It happened at a good time for me but in terms of anything else I've kind of internalised everything to enable me to stay sane.'

He is very philosophical about it all: 'For me it's just about songwriting, that's what it's all about, so anything that happens outside that, I don't mind. I have a manager and it's good when people are interested – don't get me wrong but I kinda just internalise things and worry about songwriting instead of stuff like success, in monetary or world terms.'

'The one thing I've noticed about being a songwriter; and it's something that really sticks with me, is that if you work your hardest at your songs, all that other stuff takes care of itself. Just do that as best you can and everything else is like a chain reaction. Doors open for you with good songs. There have been some really fallow, no-money times but I've been able to keep going. It's down to just furthering yourself and keeping people interested that way, rather than going down the other road and worrying about stuff that you can't control anyway.'

Naturally, receiving such high-profile praise drew attention to Richie's talent and brought many things his way: 'I basically got my manager, my label, my publisher and so many lawyers were emailing me around that time. '

An English label wanted to release 'Floating' in the UK on the back of all the buzz. ''Floating' was a bit of a disaster for me, My business acumen was non-existent and I basically ended up with only 25 per cent of 'Floating' and it's the one song everybody knows. But to be honest I don't

mind because I got stung by that in a way but hopefully I won't get stung like that again I've signed a good publishing deal now [Universal Publishing] so I'm happy enough. The publishing deal was massive for me: it was great.'

Jape signed a UK, Ireland and Europe-wide deal with V2 but when the label was bought over things were touch-and-go for a few weeks: 'I was on V2 and then V2 got bought out by Universal and then lots of bands got dropped. Luckily the A&R people who were at V2 ended up going to Co-Op, specifically one A&R girl who really liked Jape. She fought my corner and got me the deal (basically exactly the same deal just moved from V2 to Co-Op) It's all just boring business stuff!'

Jape's third album, *Ritual*, came out on V2 Co-Op in June 2008 to widespread acclaim. It featured the singles 'I Was A man', 'Strike Me Down' and 'Phil Lynott'.

Richie was lucky with touring and tour supports after *Ritual* came out. 'My manager is a cool dude [Phil Morais]. He's based in London and he manages Friendly Fires as well and he got me a good agent [CODA Music Agency] and they got me some really great festivals all around Europe.'

Jape played Glastonbury, toured with the Teenagers in Germany and Friendly Fires in the UK and got some great radio support for 'Floating' from Radio 1 DJs like Rob da Bank. Richie still found the UK a tough slog. He feels the way so many Irish bands do; that Europe is far more inviting and rewarding. 'It's quite a cynical scene over there,' says Richie. His advice to bands would be, 'Just go straight to Europe.'

'My favourite festival last year was Ola Festival in Almeria in Spain. It was really, really well run, only 25,000 people, and it was MGMT, Bjork, Digitalism and Ratatat... We were on at half seven and the place was completely rammed with loads of Spanish people who didn't have a clue who we were but we rocked it and they were fuckin' mad into it and then the backstage bar was open until 8 o'clock the next morning with free cocktails all night. It was like the middle of a desert, everybody going around in shorts and stuff, it was fuckin' cool.'

Ritual was shortlisted for the Choice Music Prize Irish album of the year 2008 and Jape won! Along with the prestige and profile came a prize fund of € 10,000. While he is grateful and appreciative it's clear that Richie hasn't let it go to his head in any way: 'To win an award is something of a blessing but in a way, you should take equal amounts of nothingness from it, just a pinch of salt scenario from the whole thing, because at the end of the day that's an award for an album I put out last year and I've moved on. I'm a different person from what I was when that came out, so to get an award for it is a little bit weird but great. I don't really attach too much importance to awards.'

'I think it's great to get nominated. I suppose if you put the album out and you worked hard on it and nobody gave a shit that'd be pretty heartbreaking. It's nice to get the nod for the shortlist. The reality of the situation is that it's still the same album that it was before it won the award so you know it doesn't make much difference!

When Richie went up to accept his award at the Choice Music Prize, he said something that struck a chord with a lot of people there on the night and it has been much spoken about and referenced since. He said: 'It's much better to be a sinking ship than a rat jumping off a sinking ship.'

Richie says it wasn't about the record industry per se: 'it wasn't really a specific thing, it was more that in life it's just better to plot your own course and if you fuckin' fail you fail. Rather than being a rat about it basically. You can apply it to many different situations but basically it's more noble to be a ship than a rat. And I think most people would know what that means. In this day and age it's becoming more important because it's harder to be a ship sometimes than a rat – just to keep your integrity and to stand up for yourself and what you know is right. There have been times with Jape – going through the whole PR thing was new to me – and there have been loads of things that I've done that I've thought, "This feels shit," and then you do it and then you look back and go, "Fuck me, what the hell was I at?" I've started to say no to things, which is a really good feeling.'

'It's a weird industry: one minute you're going around like cock of the walk with fuckin' loads of money and the next minute you're fuckin' asking your girlfriend to pay rent two months in a row! As you get older I think you learn to take the ups and the downs with the same amount of stoicism. You can't get too down and you can't be too happy either. I think the way I do it is to come up with some sort of artistic concept that I can follow through and that keeps me sane. Because I know I'm moving forward then, whereas if I'm stagnating or I'm not able to write or something, it's just a hopeless scenario.

The phenomenon of what goes up must come down is a familiar one to Richie: it's a side-effect for many entertainers, be it musicians, comedians or TV presenters but it's not widely spoken about: 'Sometimes after a gig I can get a little bit depressed, like the big gigs, especially the ones that go really well. Afterwards everyone's like, "That was fuckin' amazing," and you're just like, "Why do I feel so empty? Am I fuckin' weird?" It's true. I've spoken to some musicians about it and I think a lot of people get it; you're dancing over the abyss and then you fall into it!' he laughs. 'It's something to do with being on or something: dancing around entertaining people – and then you're a fuckin' asshole to your loved ones! It's a weird character trait…huge ego meets tiny amount of self-esteem, I think.'

Richie gets really wired before a gig: 'I get very hyper before I go onstage; everybody always says that about me. I suddenly get loads of energy and start running around the place. Just fuckin' jumping in the air and stuff: excitement and adrenalin. Yeah, I can't control myself when I go on stage, I feel really energetic. We used to have this thing called Swampys. It was rum, mint leaves, Coke, ginger ale and lime in a big drink, it was really sweet and sugary; aw, it's amazing. It's fucking beautiful!' says Richie, smiling.

As for album number four Richie has most of it written and a lot of pre-production done. He is just deciding on where to record it.

'I'm describing it as a romantic psychedelic album. That's what it is and I'm really happy with it. It took me a while. I went through writer's block after *Ritual*; I hit a wall, like, "What have I got to say now? That's everything I have to say!" So it took me a few months of just drinking loads and being depressed to realise, "Right, I need to come up with something." So I came up with the idea for the next album and I worked hard to translate that vision into an album.'

'It's a different sound but it's one I'm much more proud of than *Ritual*. I definitely know it's a better album because you're learning all the time. The thing with Jape, the one thing I'm really good at is learning from my mistakes, so I'm moving forward,' says Richie.

Jape's fourth album is due out in 2010.

Messiah J & the Expert

Artists

Messiah J
(John FitzGerald)
The Expert
(Cian Galvin)

Live Band
Glenn 'G-Bone' Keating
Paul 'Twiddler' Dunne
John 'Frankadelic' Pollard

Albums
What's Confusing You?
Now This I Have to Hear
From the Word Go

EPs
...And Another Thing

Label
Inaudible Records

Management
Shane 'General Knowledge' Galvin

Websites
www.messiahjandtheexpert.com
www.MySpace.com/messiahjandtheexpert

INTERVIEW WITH MESSIAH J [J]
AND THE EXPERT [EX]

The extraordinary thing about J and Ex is their friendship. It is at the core of everything they do. Creatively, they are completely on the same page and both are totally focused on and committed to their music. Their belief in what they do together and the energy it generates are incredibly infectious. They are genuine, decent, hard-working guys.

They have twice been shortlisted for the Choice Music Prize Irish Album of the Year. First for *Now This I Have to Hear* in 2006 and again for *From the Word Go* in 2008. They were also nominated for a Meteor Award for Best Irish Album in 2009. They have toured Ireland numerous times and played international festivals such as SXSW and Oxegen.

J and Ex met through a mutual friend, Dylan Collins, in Big Brother Records in Dublin in 1999. They were eighteen, fresh out of school, and hip-hop and music-mad. Dylan had a vision of getting all the people he knew who were passionate about hip-hop together and forming a kind of super-group. The seven member group (Messiah J, The Expert, Robbie Delaney, D.J. Splyce, D.J. Mayhem, Relevance and Grammar) were called the Stonecutters. They'd meet in the City Arts Centre and set up the decks and the mics, mess around and have fun.

'It was just kind of showing off, battling in front of one another, in a good way. Everyone showing how good they were at their individual thing,' says Ex.

'There was definitely a sense of people coming together; this common thing that you all had,' adds J.

After a couple of months of this 'coming together', Ex wanted to take things to the next level and asked two of them (Mayhem and J) if they wanted to start a band. They became Creative Controle, a name that came from the song by the rapper, O.C. ('Get your ears ready for creative control').

They started writing songs in Ex's bedroom where all the necessary gear and decks were set up, creating the kind of music that few people in Ireland were doing. 'When I was in school, there were three or four other blokes out of 120 that I could talk to about hip-hop and that was it,' Ex recalls. 'Everyone knew the Fugees, because they were massive around then, but that was as far as it went, so finding all these lads and getting off on it was huge.'

Ex's brother Shane Galvin, who now manages the band, suggested that they put together a CD and try and get some gigs. They did up five or six songs in a studio in six hours and made just thirty copies. Amongst the recipients were promoters/bookers Declan Forde and Leagues O'Toole.

'Our next practice, Dec came to watch us and he was mad into it and he said, "I wanna put on gigs just so I can see you guys," and we were like, "That sounds fuckin' great!" He brought over Mark B & Blade and that was the first show we ever played,' says Ex. It was on 27 January 2001: they both still have the poster.

High-profile support slots continued for Creative Controle. Every time a big hip-hop act came to Ireland, they were asked if they wanted to play. J remembers: 'There were three significant things that happened, one was Leagues got one [a demo CD], two was Kittser and then Eamonn Sweeney wrote about us loads as well. We were just like, "We're in the paper or a magazine?! What's this!" I think we were extremely naïve in a lovely way but we'd no idea what we were at.'

'I remember Shane, who had been plugging away in bands for years, saying, "Yis are bastards, yis have skipped the whole middle section, jumped right up a step," laughs Ex. 'We were still doing bedroom stuff on a stage basically.'

'We thought we were great!' laughs J.

Leagues O'Toole wanted to bring out a record on Volta Sounds, the label he ran with Independent Records boss, Dave O'Grady. Their first 12" was 'Bloodrush', which was a critical and radio hit.

However, their second single, 'Check The Vision', didn't go as well as hoped. 'It just kind of bombed. I think the B-side was better than the A-Side, much better,' reflects J. 'It was a song called, "Give My Right Arm".'

Creatively, the group didn't yet really know who they were. They feel that they were making music that they thought they should, rather than music from the heart. In February 2002, before the second 12" came out, J and Ex told Mayhem that they wanted to progress things without him.

'I felt so sick on the day,' remembers J. 'You're basically kicking someone out of the band: it's a horrible feeling. We just made an artistic decision, which we don't regret, with due respect to Mayhem.'

'It was horrific,' says Ex. 'It was worse than any break-up I've had, almost. We were kids; we didn't fuckin' know what we were doing. Mayhem's a dude.'

'He's a total dude,' agrees J. 'We just wanted to go more towards a band than a straight up hip-hop band. We dropped the hatchet without actually really considering what we were doing but it felt right at the time and that's all we could go on at the time.'

The name soon changed to Messiah J & The Expert.

'When I was making that first record, I was very frustrated because I knew what I wanted to do but I wasn't good enough to do it yet,' explains Ex. 'Basically, I wanted it to be what it is now: I wanted bass players, guitar players and strings but: (a) we didn't have the money; and (b) I didn't know what I was doing. Neither of us did. We were recording in studios and paying lots of money. We didn't have time to record and everything was very pressurised, I suppose. The first record was quite dark and very hip-hop.'

J agrees, describing their début as a 'very mid-tempo, intense; very hip-hop, very wordy.'

When *What's Confusing You?* came out on Volta Sounds in 2003, it had a very different sound from their first hit, 'Bloodrush': while it wasn't as angry, it wasn't particularly radio-friendly either. 'It's quite artsy actually,' says J.

'It's very artsy. It's the most artsy thing we've done!' laughs Ex in agreement.

Things changed permanently for Messiah J & the Expert in 2004, when they were offered the support slot to the Streets in Dublin Castle for the Heineken Green Energy weekend. 'For me, that was the biggest changing point for the whole band, because that gig was the biggest gig we had done to date and it was the first gig we'd ever done with a band. We got a great response that day,' says Ex.

Messiah J & the Expert didn't do another record with Volta Sounds: 'It didn't interest us and it didn't interest them: it was one of these unsaid things, where it was just like, "We're not going to do another one. Fair play, it's been nice,"' explains J.

Ex had studied sound engineering in Coláiste Dhulaigh, a course that paid off tremendously for him and the band: 'We bought ProTools so that we could record at home and that was a huge moment in the band.'

It was in their home studio that they recorded a three-song demo in the hope of finding a new label deal. The first track was 'Something Outta Nothing', a fresh, new sound for the band.

Highly respected and influential BBC Radio 1 DJ, Steve Lamacq, liked the demo a lot: 'He was playing an unmastered, completely rough demo of our single and he brought us over for a session and we were like, "That's a bit mad!"' remembers J.

Steve Lamacq was not the only one to be taken with 'Something Outta Nothing'. Fellow DJs at the BBC, Mike Davies and Steve Merchant, played it, as did J. Kennedy of Xfm. Things were looking good for Messiah J & the Expert but it wasn't translating into the label deal they wanted.

'There was a lot of, "Oh we want someone to sign us," remembers J, 'But then in true DIY spirit, we just said, "Shag that, no one's going to sign us, we've got to do it ourselves; we believe in ourselves."'

Their manager Shane encouraged them to set up their own label, Inaudible Records. The first release on Inaudible was the 12", 'When the Bull Gores the Matador', in March 2006. 'That was a massively clever decision for ourselves because we would have been waiting for a bus that wasn't going to come,' admits J.

Their second album, *Now This I Have to Hear*, came out in October 2006 with a series of popular singles and was shortlisted for the Choice Music Prize Irish Album of the Year 2006. 'At the time, it was a bit of a shock because we thought: 'Ah, the aul' dinosaurs won't get it, because a lot of the Irish music industry is quite old, so I suppose it was great, like "Holy shit, maybe new music can make a breakthrough!"' says Ex.

They toured nationally, with numerous headline shows and high-profile supports, including playing support to Public Enemy in Tripod. By now, Messiah J & the Expert's audience had grown much wider and included indie, pop and dance fans, in addition to the hip-hop fans they started with.

Messiah J & the Expert operate a true DIY ethos. J, Ex and Shane run the band and the label almost like a charitable organisation: any profits from gigs go back into the pot to pay for future expenses.

'We never, ever took a penny from any gig and that has financed everything,' states Ex. 'I think that's a good philosophy to have, because

sometimes you think, "I've played a gig, I've worked hard I want at least fifty quid," but then down the line you're like, "We need that new piece of gear," and you've nothing to buy it with.'

The practicalities of a band cost money: simple basics like rehearsal space, travel and PR. There is never enough. 'We are actually very sensible with money overall and I don't think we could change that because if we squander it all, we can't do stuff that's going to take the band to another level,' explains J.

'Loads of bands I know are hugely in debt, so not to be in debt is like a miracle,' says Ex.

Messiah J & the Expert really want to spend their time touring and promoting themselves outside Ireland. More than anything else, they want to be able to do this full-time.

'It's an obsession,' states J. 'We're looking at the UK. We are not happy just being good in an Irish context, just being an Irish band. If we were going to settle for that, we might as well give up now.'

'That's when money actually becomes really important," Ex notes. 'You go over there and you like to think the music can get you as far as it will but it won't: money's important. For *Now This I've Got to Hear*, we actually did go to England and we only played one gig but we got PR and spent a shitload of cash and it was disastrous.'

The PR company the band had retained turned out to be a massive disappointment and money down the drain. 'We basically made a mistake going with them but it's all in hindsight,' sighs J. '

'That's our horror story,' admits Ex.

Money is a frustration for Messiah J & The Expert, as it is for so many bands. 'I, being arrogant, think if we had loads of money pumped into us we could be doing way better than some of the

IN BLOOM - MESSIAH J & THE EXPERT

bands out there: the problem is getting that chance, and it sucks, but money is *so* important; and it's *shit*!' groans Ex. 'If we had the money, we'd fuckin' use it way better than most bands: that's for damn sure.'

'But then you have to look at the silver lining in everything and the DIY attitude stands to you for life, not just music: life,' believes J. 'Taking things into your own hands is just invaluable.'

Their third album, *From the Word Go,* came out in October 2008 to rave reviews. It features additional lead vocals from Leda Egri on the single 'Turn The Magic On', Joanne Daly on 'Amnesia Comes Easily' and Ro and Kieran from Delorentos on 'Geography'. It brought them a second shortlist for the Choice Music Prize Irish Album of the Year and a 2009 Meteor Award nomination for Best Irish Album.

'What I think is remarkable about the album is that it is eclectic and you can have happy, shake-your-booty stuff but then there's some serious social issues and hard-ass stuff in there as well, musically,' says J.

'I couldn't be more proud of it,' announces Ex. 'I'm 95, no, more like 98 per cent over the moon with it: absolutely. I wouldn't really change anything.'

'I wouldn't change anything but I do think we can go better again,' says J.

While they're justifiably proud of *From the Word Go*, they do admit to having had some doubts about the reaction it would get from fans and critics alike, as Ex explains: 'We honestly thought because it was so eclectic, no one's going to get it; people will think half the album's great – what's the other half about?'

'We were just going, "Have we created a monster or have we created a good album?" I've never felt so numb towards our music. I think that was purely a symptom of having just put *everything* into it,' says J.

Messiah J & the Expert were pleasantly surprised by their subsequent Meteor Award nomination: 'When Shane emailed it to us we thought it was a joke. Look who we were up against: Snow Patrol – with hundreds of thousands put into their album – or the Script. Our album cost about three grand! That's what's so great about it, really,' says Ex.

'For me, the most important thing is the album and its being as timeless as possible,' notes Ex. 'That's my main priority, that I can go back in five years' time and just go, "That's really good."'

'That's what you're buried with,' summarises J. 'They'll remember shows but that's the document.'

Ex agrees wholeheartedly. 'Yeah, that's it, and I want the document to be as close to perfect as possible: that's *always* my main goal.'

'I was doing an interview recently and I was asked, "So what do you want; the musos or the masses?" recounts J. 'And I was like, "Both please!" That is my attitude because we're not trying to be elitist with what we are doing.'

Ex agrees: 'Good music is good music.'

Mundy

Artist
Mundy
(Edmund Enright)

Albums
Jelly Legs
24 Star Hotel
Raining Down Arrows
Live and Confusion
Strawberry Blood

EP
The Moon Is a Bullet Hole
(Camcor Recording)

Label
Camcor Recording

Management
Dave O'Grady

Websites
www.mundy.ie
www.MySpace.com/mundyirl

Mundy has a friendly twinkle, a hint of devilment in his eyes. He laughs like the bold boy in school whom everyone likes, including the teachers. He's great company: he is a fun, down-to-earth, unpretentious guy. Mundy doesn't care about what is trendy or about trying to be cool: he just plays the kind of music he loves and puts huge energy and enthusiasm into his performances. He's passionate about music and has a very wide range of tastes and influences, easily winning people over with his songwriting and his on-stage charm.

He has multiple platinum records, including the Number 1 album, *Raining Down Arrows*, numerous Top 20 hits, and a Meteor Award for the most downloaded song of 2008: 'Galway Girl', with Sharon Shannon.

Mundy's parents run a pub in Birr, County Offaly, and there was always a lot of music playing. Not live music – the pub had an eight-track machine. 'Simon and Garfunkel would have been huge and the Bee Gees and all that kind of stuff,' Mundy smiles as he recalls the size of the old cassettes. 'It was like putting a video into it!'

Mundy's aunts were also really into music, which had a big impact on his young ears. They had loads of vinyl and diverse tastes: the Rolling Stones, the Beatles, Bill Hailey and the Comets, Elvis, the Royal Show Band, Roy Orbison: 'I guess I was around a lot of music and I never knew I loved it but I was always listening to it.'

Mundy got his own bedroom at the age of four or five and remembers: 'We had a one-speaker cassette player in the house with a radio on it and I used to bring that up to my bedroom and I used to listen to ABBA. I had a pink Elvis Presley cassette but I can't remember which album that was!'

'My parents bought my brother and myself a guitar when I was five and I used to write out the lyrics to the songs, as much as I could, and finger off and try and play – I think it was open tuning,' he recalls. 'So I was really into it, passionate about it, for about six months, and then I gave it up altogether.'

At that stage, Mundy was getting into swimming in a big way (he swam for Offaly twice) and that took up most of his time between the age of six and twelve. He was also really big into GAA and horse-riding and rode until he was seventeen: 'I never had my own horse but I used to work in a yard that had stables and lots of horses.'

It wasn't until he was about fourteen that music started to come back into the picture: 'A priest called Pat Gilbert came to the school, bringing with him a bass amp, a bass, drum kit, a guitar and guitar amp. He just came out of nowhere, wearing a leather jacket and a collar, and he was the coolest-looking priest ever! He set up a band for the school Mass. Older friends of Mundy's were in the band and he thought they sounded amazing. 'So myself and my friends in my class decided to get the old guitars that we were given as kids restrung.'

They formed their first school band that year with two guitars, a bass and drums but no singer. 'I ended up being the singer because there was no one to join the band, I had no choice really. I always imagined that I'd find the singer and then I could stand back.'

'We were called Stage Fright,' declares a grinning Mundy. 'The first song we wrote was called "Confusion," he laughs. 'We were quite serious about it and we loved it. I had a rehearsal room called the hippy heaven and it was just posters of Bob Dylan and Neil Young and I had a record player in there and I used to play everything and anything: Horslips, Thin Lizzy, Deep Purple.'

Then at sixteen the other band that was first set up in school came calling: 'They wanted me to join and they were doing better, so I left Stage Fright and I joined Blind Vision.' Mundy cackles with laughter at the recollection of his mercenary behaviour. 'All of a sudden, we were playing in pubs and getting money.'

Mundy had little interest in study that year. He was still into horses but music was taking over. He did his Leaving Cert and passed but, not being a straight-A student, he decided to move to Dublin, where he started busking. 'My parents thought I was doing a sound engineering course,' confesses Mundy. 'I told them I was doing sound engineering in Ballyfermot but I was doing the rock school. I lied to them for a whole year and when I got back, I remember being in bed in the summer holidays and my dad came into the room screaming, "You're the biggest liar ever, you've being lying to us for a whole year!"'

They hadn't wanted him to do the course because there was nothing at the end of it: 'At least at the end of the sound engineering course, there was a chance of working in RTÉ or an advertising agency and that's what I was going on about all the time.'

Mundy was making up stories about soundtracks they were working on and all sorts. He passed his exams but he didn't find the rock school very useful for him: 'The whole time I was meant to be out there [in college] I was busking. I found out about Dave Murphy: he was running a night in McDaids every Tuesday night, that's where I saw Glen Hansard for the first time. Also Bronagh Gallagher, Mark Dignam, Maria Doyle Kennedy, Angeline Ball – *The Commitments* peak was over at that time but everyone was still famous.'

For musicians, McDaids closed up shop but the songwriting nights started again the following week in the International Bar: 'I asked your man if I could get up and play a song and that's when it really started for me.'

Mundy absorbed all he could from those nights: 'I really began to listen a lot, looked and learned as to how songs were built in the International, then I started writing "Gin and Tonic Sky" and those songs. Dave Murphy told me that a couple of people from Sony had been coming in and out every Tuesday wondering if I was on. I had no idea this was going on. I'd met Hazel O'Connor around this stage and Hazel asked me to play the guitar with her and she had a friend Sally Ann who was English, who wanted to manage bands. She saw me play in the International and said, "I want to manage you," and I said, "OK."'

Mundy demoed ten songs and gave his manager the tape and she took it back to England, where interest peaked immediately: 'The publishing guy came over straight away and a guy from Sony came over straight away. They wanted to sign me and I was like, "I'm kind of only messing here," or, "I'm not ready for this."'

'Before I signed the publishing deal I was told to come over to London to play for EMI in their office,' he remembers. 'The publishing deal was with Warner Chapel but EMI wanted to hear my songs. I had made the demo at this stage but it was very basic, so they flew me over and I got a lend of a guitar and I sat in their boardroom and played in front of six or seven people. It was insane! I sat in PolyGram's boardroom as well and I did that for about four different labels: that's a real old school thing, to actually play in front of labels.'

A frenzy of interest followed: 'Anything that they took interest in was serious, so everyone – Mother Records, RCA, name any of them, they all took me for dinner. It was a head fuck!' recalls Mundy. 'Absolutely nuts. I was only nineteen at the time and I was being told that I was an amazing singer and amazing songwriter. Smoke was being blown up my ass a lot by all these strangers, not by Irish people. I was shitting myself.'

It was an incredibly stressful scenario for a teenager to find himself in and Mundy is honest about how scary it got for him. 'I started having panic attacks around then. I'd had a few before that but these were definitely worse.' This was before mobile phones so Mundy's parents didn't even know what was going on, it was all being organised through his management.

'I decided on Epic Records. S2 offered me an eight-album deal but they could drop me after every album. Epic offered me a six-album deal with two firm, so they couldn't drop me after the first one.'

It seemed a better option to Mundy at the time, so the lawyers were brought in. Everything moved very quickly then. Mundy was on tour with Alanis Morrisette within weeks of signing his deal. Next he was in Wales recording his début album, *Jelly Legs*, with critically acclaimed producer Youth: 'It was insane, it was all very fast.'

'I had the biggest agent in the UK,' begins Mundy. 'I was on the front page of *Music Week* and it was fucking like, "the next Bruce Springsteen, next Bob Dylan, next Kurt Cobain, next Michael Stipe, *next everything*!" I was the next everything,' says Mundy, shaking his head in disbelief.

These are comparisons many would dream of but nearly impossible to live up to: 'I remember doing a gig on Bournemouth on one of the tours and this guy came up to me and said, "You're nothing like Michael Stipe," and I was like, "I didn't say that I was."'

The backlash at home soon followed: 'The press in Dublin slated me. I was signed to England, not to anyone in Ireland, so the Irish people were like, "Who the hell is this guy and what's the big fuss about?" So I had to go and prove myself then.' The label didn't want Mundy spending his time in Ireland, so he toured the UK around six times, France seven times and enjoyed a couple of tours around the US.

"To You I Bestow" was licensed for inclusion on the soundtrack for Baz Luhrmann's adaptation of William Shakespeare's *Romeo and Juliet*. Nellee Hooper, who was composing the soundtrack, had rung up and asked for a few tracks. The label gave him three songs and he picked 'To You I Bestow'. 'That was an amazing thing,' admits Mundy. The soundtrack for the film went on to sell eleven million copies, going gold and platinum all over the world.

The good news was soon followed by frustration. 'When "To You I Bestow" was released as a single, it was the highest radio add-on in college radio in America. It was the fourth highest overall ('Discotheque' was the highest) and there wasn't one single in the shop. Then the shops got flooded but it was too late. Then it came out on *Romeo and Juliet* and they wouldn't re-release it as a single. It took me about five years to get the guts to break my management deal after that... it was fucking painful.'

The whole experience left Mundy a little jaded: 'It's hard to trust people. I had to tell one of the guys in the record label to tell people to stop kissing me and hugging me, because I didn't know any of them. It was spinning my head out.'

It's funny for him now as he mimics their accents: '"Awright, babes! Awright?" Ahhh, get away from me!' he laughs.

The man who had signed Mundy told him to move over to London to start on the second album: 'The week I moved over and signed a lease for a house, he left the record label. So I had no A&R guy and I'd signed a twelve-grand lease for a year.'

After a few more headaches Mundy recorded his second album, *24 Star Hotel*, in 1999, only to be dropped by his record company in 2000. 'I rang up the lawyers to see if I could get the album back and they said I hadn't been officially dropped yet (even though they told my manager that I had been dropped) because they hadn't bothered to do the paperwork. It took about a year and a half,' laughs Mundy. 'So I couldn't even talk to other labels because I was still signed.'

It is an awful story, a story that Mundy knows he shares with many other people. But he has moved on and found success on his own, independently. 'I'm over it but that's why I haven't really gone out and looked for a deal,' he explains.

The career Mundy has in Ireland today started when he was dropped: 'I started seeing the Frames going out and doing their own thing. Loads of bands were doing it. So I started booking gigs all over the country. It was back to basics!'

Mundy was playing small venues like the Lobby, the Róisín Dubh and the Stables. The turn-out was good and Mundy soon noticed people were singing his new songs back to him: 'I said I'd do a single, an EP and then an album. "Mexico" and "July" were a double A-side and then I had the EP with "Mayday" on it, *The Moon Is a Bullet Hole*.'

Mundy formed his own label and called it after the river that runs through Birr, Camcor. He started small, printing 500 singles, and followed those with 4,000 albums. *24 Star Hotel* finally got its release on Camcor in 2002. 'It really crawled out the door – it didn't take off at all, initially,' remembers Mundy. *24 Star Hotel* went into the charts at Number 9 and went on to sell 50,000 copies.

'I think I had to earn my stripes,' he stresses. 'I felt I had to prove myself and show that I could play and I think I did. Any opportunity I had to play in front of people, I treated it as a life or death situation. I really felt that it was at a time when I could fall flat on my face or I could really set off my career again.'

"July" was the song that did it for Mundy, becoming a huge hit. Its sister A-side, "Mexico" was a hit with radio and fans as well but 'July' got an extra lease of life through a later, faster, live recording.

Raining Down Arrows, Mundy's third album, went straight into the Irish charts at Number 1. He recorded it with Mark Addison in Austin, Texas, in 2003, a place he had visited many times and fallen in love with. Mundy toured France, Holland and the UK with the album and it was released in Australia and New Zealand on Little Big Music. With Mundy already a live favourite, the success of the album solidified his position as a major headline attraction in Ireland, with *Raining Down Arrows* eventually reaching platinum sales.

Mundy's popularity would lead him to perform a duet of sorts, one that would go on to create another massive hit, a cover of Steve Earle's 'Galway Girl'.

The story goes: 'Tom Dunne was doing a live broadcast and Sharon [Shannon] and I were both in on the show and he asked if I would learn the words to 'Galway Girl' and sing it with Sharon. After that it was like, "Will I play that again? That sounded great." I started doing it with her whenever we'd meet up and then Ray D'Arcy got us in to do it. I got her on to do the Vicar Street thing [the recording of his album *Live and Confusion*].'

Mundy's live version with Sharon from *Live and Confusion* became a Number 1 download and it stayed in the top spot for weeks: '"Galway Girl" was never released as a single by me,' explains Mundy. With download charts, you don't have to officially release something: it's just calculated on sales.'

Having one song take off in such an extraordinary way can sometimes be a bad thing, (especially when you didn't write it and won't benefit from royalties) as it can eclipse your body of work: 'It's a curse and a blessing,' he confesses. 'Meeting Sharon Shannon was a blessing and I knew Shane McGowan but I didn't know him as well and I met Mike Scott again.'

Mundy guested with Sharon Shannon's Big Band on tour in the UK: 'Steve Earle got up and sang it with me at the Cambridge Folk Festival. Loads of things have happened as a result of it. I was asking him to sing it with me in Ireland when I was in Cambridge but he said he couldn't do it, that he had to fly away. Then I was singing "July" at the Midlands festival the next day and I started singing "Galway Girl" and I turned around and there he was, fucking singing the second verse! Amazing.'

IN BLOOM - MUNDY

'So some great things have happened but the weird thing is, that's all some people know me for. But then I played Oxegen last year [2008], and there were probably 10,000 people there and they knew all my songs, so that made me feel better.'

Mundy recorded *Strawberry Blood* in August 2008. 'I couldn't wait to get into the studios to do something new and something more down my street. There is a country twinge in what I do but there are pop elements and rock elements. It all got a bit mixed up when I went on the road with Sharon: so I really had to get back to that. I was just dying to get back into the studio and make some feedback, and make some noise and experiment with sound and stuff. I spent a fortune on it – I think you should spend what it needs to make something beautiful.'

'Waiting for the Night to Come' was an instant radio hit and *Strawberry Blood* went into the charts at fourteen. 'Cruising Paradise' followed, a perfect summer anthem for Mundy to hit the festivals with. The third single from Strawberry Blood, 'The Corn And The Orange Sun' was released on October 23, 2009 with instant radio play and positive press.

Mundy's eyes are set further afield these days, with a new agent in the UK, Australian and UK tours booked and France high on the agenda: 'My whole thing is to get the hell out of here. It always has been but it just never happened.'

As for the near future, Mundy dreams of touring a show with all his friends involved. 'Personally I'd love to do what Springsteen did with *The Seeger Sessions*, I'd love to do a version of that, where there's Irish in it but it's nearly punky, it's nearly like the Pogues with a Springsteen edge to it. Everybody would want to be in the band at some point. If someone had to go off and do their own thing, you could get someone else to step in, like Dylan's Rolling Thunder Revue. I'd love to do this. I just have to find the right time.'

Republic of Loose

Band Members

Mik Pyro (Michael Tierney)
Dave Pyro (Dave Haughton)
Deco (Declan Quinn)
Brez (Cormac Breslin)
Benjamin Loose
   (Daniel Benjamin Marcus)
Andre Antunes (Andre Lopes)

Currently featured with the Loose:

Orla La (Orla Breslin);
Emily Rose (Emily Aylmer)

Albums

This Is the Tomb of the Juice
Aaagh!
Vol IV: Johnny Pyro and the Dance of Evil

Label

Loaded Dice Records

Management

Dermot Doran

US Management

Asti Management

Websites

www.republicofloose.com
www.MySpace.com/republicofloose

MIK PYRO AND BENJAMIN LOOSE (ALSO REFERED TO AS PODGE BY MIK) REPRESENTED THE BAND FOR THE INTERVIEW.

The Republic of Loose are cool. Many try to be – they work at it, contrive it, style it or copy it – the Loose just have it. They have their own unique thing going on: a sound that is so different from anything else in Ireland (and arguably anywhere else). Mik Pyro's voice and range are enviable. The band are funky, soulful, dirty – a mix of pop, rock, r'n'b, blues, even hip-hop. They are unlike the rest, their own little republic, you could say, and if they are loose it's only because they are so at the top of their game musically that they can have fun with it. They make it look effortless, which means they have worked really hard and clocked up the hours. They have three albums, the first released on an English indie label, the others self-released on their own Loaded Dice Records.

Republic of Loose won Hope For 2004 at the Meteor Ireland Music Awards and were shortlisted for the 2006 Choice Music Prize for *Aaagh!*. They have played Oxegen numerous times, supported U2 in Croke Park, and were part of the Arthur's Day celebrations (250th birthday of Guinness) in October 2009.

Front man Mik started playing in bands when he was about twelve, having had years of classical guitar and piano lessons through his childhood: 'I did my first gig when I was thirteen. I was always in metal bands growing up.'

Mik met Dave through a mutual friend, sowing the seeds for their own musical revolution. Dave used to have parties in Churchtown, where people would be jamming, playing the blues. It was at those parties that he really got to know Dave and met Brez. Soon after, Mik and Dave started jamming together and got seriously into blues and soul music. Then they started writing their own material and began playing together. They came up with the name Johnny Pyro and the Rock Coma ahead of a gig.

Mik was in his early twenties at this stage and had previously been playing a lot of music he didn't really like: 'I was playing in a lot of shitty rock bands. I was caught in some kind of cultural vacuum – I wasn't really playing the music I wanted to play: I was playing a lot of shite. It was what I thought the hot chicks in UCD were into that year or whatever. It was a bit stupid.'

Mik got back into playing the blues and started listening to the Wu Tang Clan. The challenge for him personally became to find a way to bridge the gap between the music he liked and the music he was playing.

'I was scared to use any of that kind of information in the music. I was always into blues and into soul and hip-hop but trying to apply that to the music we were doing rather than just listening to it. I never had the balls to apply it. I thought, "You can't do that, that's *their* music, that's over there." It was when I broke through that fear barrier of trying to apply the sound of some of the music that I actually liked into the rock musicianship that we'd inherited, – that's when it started getting kind of interesting musically.'

Johnny Pyro became like the house band in Eamon Dorans, where the band met their manager Dermot Doran. Benjamin remembers watching them before he was even in the band. While still in Johnny Pyro, Mik played in a country band with his sister Annie, called Rats of the Shining Path. Benjamin was playing bass in the band, so when a couple of guys left Johnny Pyro, they asked him to join. They knew Brez already, so he was next.

'We knew he was one of the best guitar players around. He was a good friend of Dave's and he had come to a few gigs and he liked them, so when the other guitar player left we asked Brez to join and he said, "Yeah."'

It was only when they got a deal with the UK record company Big Cat that they became the Republic of Loose. They had been doing gigs with the new members as Johnny Pyro but Benjamin says the label owner wanted them to change their name.

'He said he thought it was too confusing because people thought that Mik was Johnny Pyro. The idea was that Johnny Pyro was a mythical character who informed us but we'd be like, "Where's Johnny?" and he thought that this was just too complicated an idea!'

The whole thing is very funny to both of them, Mik laughs: 'God forbid that I'd be perceived as a leader.'

Apparently when they told him the new name, the response was not positive: 'Sounds like a football team.'

'Yeah, he was pissed off,' Benjamin laughs. "He got into it in the end, though.'

Mik says the name was pretty instinctive and it turned out to be appropriate that they changed their name as their sound evolved with the new members.

'I just liked the sound of the words but it was pretty fitting that we came up with that name. When Brez and Deco came in (Deco was a mate of Brez) we started shifting into a bit more r'n'b territory. We were listening to a lot more contemporary r'n'b from the 1980s which people didn't listen to at all because they thought it was naff or cheesy or whatever – we always kind of liked that music. We were listening to Timbaland but I think we really started to be able to play it properly only when Brez and Deco joined. So then the sound of the band starting shifting and we were moving away from a gospel-y, bluesy type thing to a more r'n'b, soul type of thing.'

The name has always seemed fitting for the band as a way of acknowledging their difference from the other Dublin bands of the time. Republic of Loose were based in Eamon Dorans when a lot of the other musicians seemed to be in Whelans. Benjamin thinks that their hanging out in a different place helped the band become who they are.

'There were people getting signed out of Whelans and they were getting features written about them and they were getting deals, so I think everyone in Dublin gravitated towards that… but we used that, in a sense, to define ourselves

as *not* that. I remember Dave slagging off the Frames in an interview and shit like that, stupid stuff but at the time it was helpful in discovering our own identity. Like what Mik was talking about before: the idea of the band was always to use different kinds of references and the Whelans bands were all kind of using more traditional references. So it was kind of like you define yourself in part by who you are and in other part by who you're not – and we weren't them. So we kind of cultivated that, if only in our own minds, to help build our own identity and that kind of separateness.'

Mik didn't have anything against the Whelans' scene but Dorans was *their* scene: it became their territory.

'It was just a kind of separate energy anyway, Dorans was over there and it was just a bar and it did kind of become a locus for an awful lot of stuff. We just used to play blues gigs in there: we wouldn't rehearse or anything – we'd just go in and play blues. It was where we hung out all the time and there was a lot of madness. We ended up putting our rehearsal room up there as well and our manager ran the bar and we'd be down in Voodoo, so it was like we had our own little set-up. It was good for fermenting that kind of sense of a gang or a sense of a unit.'

This Is the Tomb of the Juice came out in 2004 on Big Cat records and was released in the UK and Ireland to good reviews. The album was a mix of songs from the Johnny Pyro days and newer Republic of Loose material. Mik knows some of the songs were very good but he feels that they didn't execute them properly, as they were just starting to feel their way into a more r'n'b sound. He laughingly recalls their experience with the image-led UK music scene:

'It was very hard for anybody to market it, especially with the way we looked on top of that. I don't know why anyone would have signed us,

© TARA MCCORMACK

to be honest. I think they took one look at me and thought, "No matter what you do with that fucker you're wasting your time!"'

Joking aside, Mik feels it's radio that has saved them, both in Ireland and the UK. 'We're not the kind of band that appeals to journalists, really. We don't hit a lot of the right references, so if you don't appeal to the *NME* or whatever, it can be a bit of a hard slog. We make kind of weird music because it's a composite of so many different things and it's almost like everything's sandwiched on top of each other. We don't really make cohesive statements in terms of albums. There's a lot of different information going on so it's difficult for anyone to get their head around it. It's difficult for *us* to get our heads around it sometimes.'

Mik feels that they have ended up being perceived by some people as a commercial band due to their success with radio but that was never their intention. They endured a lot of abuse for their perceived commercialism.

'People were really vitriolic in their hatred towards us,' Mik recalls. 'Now nobody gives a shit but if I was walking down the street any given week I could have people shouting abuse at me: "You're fuckin' shit" – that kind of thing. You get a lot of people saying nice things as well but you don't remember them.'

When the time came for album number two, one of their demos, 'Comeback Girl' ended up sounding so good that they decided to put the single out to radio to help keep their profile up. The song became a massive hit. Benjamin remembers their surprise: 'We had no idea that was going to happen. If we knew that was going to happen we would have had an album to put out a month later but we didn't have an album ready: it was a year or more before we put the album out.'

'I remember doing a gig in Ennis and there were 150 people there and we played the whole gig and not one person moved from the wall. Then we played 'Comeback Girl' and they all legged it into the middle: it was a first-time experience. Up until then, we had a hardcore following and apart from that, we couldn't really gig that much, like most bands.'

Some of their hardcore following were put out by the band's new-found success. 'There were people who would come up and go, "You fuckin' betrayed us,"' says Benjamin. 'People who loved the first one and loved the grimey, gospel-y rock stuff and thought we'd sold out. But nothing happened by design.'

'That's always been the way with us,' admits Mik. 'Our crowd seems to keep shifting. There seems to be new people coming in with every album and then other people leave.'

One obvious benefit for the lads was the fact that, 'More females started coming to the gigs,' laughs Mik. After that we just wanted to make pop songs!'

Benjamin smiles in agreement: 'Yeah we couldn't have got spat on, on the first album!'

Being a newly independent band (their deal with Big Cat was for one album only), they spent the next few months gigging, to raise money for studio time. The result, *Aaagh!* (silent 'g') was released on their own Loaded Dice Records in 2006 and was shortlisted for the Choice Music Prize Irish Album of the Year.

The independent route may mean more hassle and more headaches but the end results are worth it, Benjamin explains: 'We gave ourselves more of a budget than any band that's signed to a major label here in Ireland would be given, so you have that freedom, and you have the reward that you make five or six euro a record.' He also jokes that he loves walking around thinking, 'I'm the CEO of Loaded Dice Records!'

On a serious note, he feels that, 'The old model of signing to a major label and all that is just bullshit: it's bankrupt and it doesn't work to the band's advantage. They could have signed a three-album deal, they might not even have got the first one out and they're stuck in the deal. You literally don't have a move to make except for breaking up the band and beginning under a different name. So I think we're blessed: we've managed to avoid some of the clichéd hells.'

Mik nods. 'I've seen the horror: just the idea that someone could stop you making a record, stop you releasing it, on their whim…'

This explains why they didn't really pursue any of the interest from major labels, following the success of 'Comeback Girl' and *Aaagh!*

Mick says, 'Like life is too short to be talking to morons and letting them tell you how to make an album. Being a huge rock star or whatever is not really the important aspect of it: the important aspect of it is if you're an artist or a musician. You want to be able to make the music you want to make. You don't want to be dealing with people who haven't a fuckin' clue what they're talking about.'

Republic of Loose have always been known for the quality of their live shows, so one naturally wonders if nerves still play a part or if they have to hype themselves up before a show to kick-start their adrenalin. For Mik, it's a bit of both.

'The band is so tight now, a lot of the time I just have to listen to them…It's almost like I'm doing karaoke sometimes. I feel like I'm actually going out to sing these hits with this band behind me. The better the band gets, the better we all get as musicians, the more it becomes like play, more

like fun. It's not really like hard work any more. I've realised more in the last few years that it's very important to be relaxed at the start of a gig, especially when you're not fit. When I get excited on stage, either through nerves or a big crowd or something, I just tend to go fuckin' nuts, and when I go nuts, I run out of breath and then I can't sing for the rest of the gig.'

Republic of Loose work hard: 'We take gigs very seriously and we take very seriously trying not to look as though we take them very seriously!' admits Benjamin.

The band have had a lot of highlights in their career so far, supporting U2 in Croke Park, playing with Snow Patrol and all the big festivals. Benjamin thinks about some of the big moments for him and for the band: 'Playing with John Prine in England or playing with the Neville Brothers in the Ambassador – amazing things you'll remember for ever. Playing to 30,000 people at Oxegen: stuff like that is incredible. Following the Wu Tang around for three days at T in the Park.'

'In Ireland, just knowing that your music really means stuff to people is an amazing reward… Meeting kids on the street who are screaming at you and seeing kids posting stuff up on YouTube with them and their mates in their gaff going nuts to your stuff, that's kind of meaningful stuff.'

Mik: 'We played Oxegen one time – I think it was on the big stage – and just during 'Break', I was jumping, and just seeing everybody jump, it was like I'd some vision in my head of when I was a kid, imagining you're Freddie Mercury or something. Seeing that was like proof of concept, in a lot of ways. Even when we played Crawdaddy and the whole crowd sang the lyrics to 'Hold Up' – because that was the first album I'd put out and I'd written those lyrics – for the crowd to be singing them back at me, that's a fuckin' great thing. That's what you're doing it for. It was great to work with Styles P: that's another highlight. He's just a genius with language. He's one of the best rappers in New York so it was a real honour to fuckin' do a song with him.'

'We've had an awful lot of fun. There's been some shite as well but there have definitely been a lot of adventures over the last seven years. I wouldn't change it for the world, 'cos it's been interesting.'

Some of the Loose's most interesting adventures have been in the US, where their unique musical hybrid seems most at home.

'When we play the States, we seem to get on very well compared to Britain and even Ireland,' Mik admits. 'When we first started playing [in Ireland], people'd be like, "What the fuck?" I suppose it's because we listen to a lot of American music, so our music is very influenced by that. In terms of industry, we seem to get a better vibe in the States as well.'

The band have an American management deal with Kristi Clifford from Asti management, who numbers a host of hip-hop acts amongst her clientèle, including New York rapper, Styles P. She has a few deals on the table for them but is hoping for something substantial, as few indie deals have the money necessary to market, promote and tour an album properly in the USA. As owners of their own material, they also have the option of a licensing deal. Whatever they decide on, it looks like the Republic of Loose will be spending more time there touring. Mik says they will probably make a compilation of the three albums (take all the hits) for their first Stateside release.

'I'd love people outside this country to hear our music: that's an aspiration of mine. But we've no illusions. These days, you can have a career without making a spectacular splash – especially the way things are going with the Internet and the way people buy music now and how people make money out of music: it's a different industry from what it was years ago.'

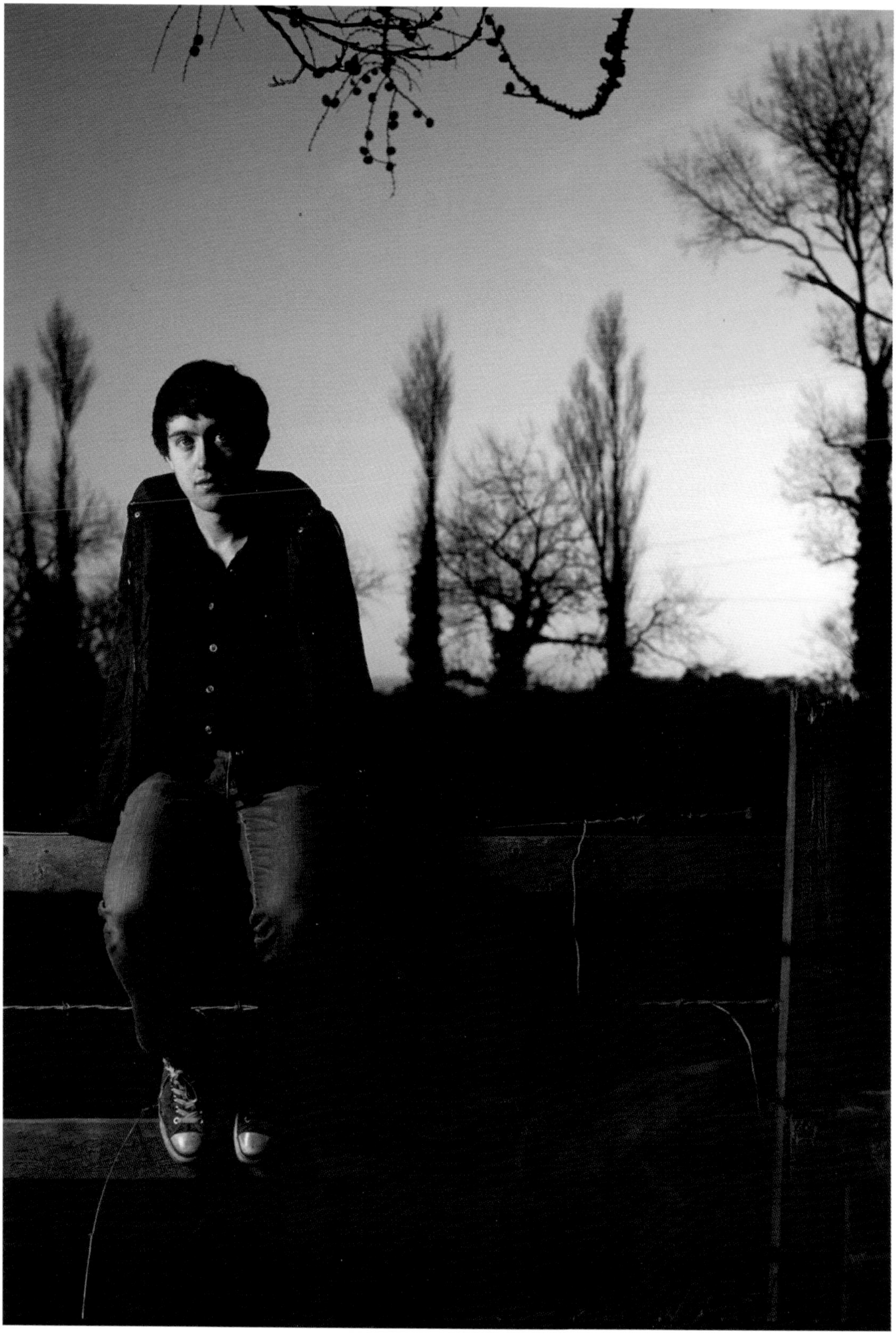

© RICHARD GILLIGAN

Villagers

Artist
Conor J. O'Brien

Live Band
Tommy McLaughlin
James Byrne
Cormac Curran
Danny Snow

EP
Hollow Kind

7" Single
'On a Sunlit Stage'

Label
Double Six Records

Management
Darrin Robson, FP Music

Websites
www.MySpace.com/wearevillagers

In person, Conor O'Brien is soft-spoken and unassuming – a mix of friendly shyness and musical assuredness. On stage, he has enviable presence and charisma: all eyes are on him. Conor has that *thing* that is so hard to describe that it's known by a single letter. He is a remarkably talented musician.

Conor is a multi-instrumentalist, singer, songwriter and artist. Following the demise of the much loved band the Immediate, in which he played a key part, Conor played with Cathy Davey, touring with her as guitarist in her band while working on his own music. Conor's music arrived to the public in late 2008, via MySpace, as Villagers.

Villagers is usually a full band live but it can also be Conor solo. The début Villagers EP, *Hollow Kind*, released in February 2009, showed a range of sweet, fragile, melodies and creative arrangements, combined with crashing, dissonant guitars and drums, all brought together by a voice that shows vulnerability and emotion. Conor's music had fans instantly.

Hollow Kind had the music industry talking and word spread quickly from Ireland to the UK. Agents, labels and publishers all wanted to hear more. A sold-out show in Whelans was followed by a UK and Irish tour with Bell X 1, supports to Neil Young and Tracy Chapman and festival appearances at Oxegen, Latitude and Electric Picnic.

During a whirlwind of activity Conor signed a publishing deal with Domino Publishing in September 2009 and signed to their Double Six Records label. An Irish single release and tour kept momentum going while Villagers début full-length was recorded [due out on Double Six in early 2010].

Conor's childhood was not musical in the way that you might expect. He took piano lessons when he was very young but it was his older brother's love of rock music that stimulated Conor's passion for creating music.

'My parents don't play any music. My Dad likes Sinatra and stuff – he *half*-likes music – but they don't really know much about music. My brother played guitar and that was my main thing, because he used to listen to Pink Floyd *constantly*, so there was this weird psychedelic music going on. He pretty much learned all the guitar solos off by heart' – he's a really good guitarist. He's probably a bit out of practice now he's but an awesome guitarist. He showed me the chords when I was about twelve,' says Conor.

'My main music memory is of his giving me *Pink Floyd: Live at Pompeii* [1972], the footage of them playing in a real amphitheatre in Pompeii (it was in the 1970s and it was before *Dark Side Of The Moon*, around the time of *Meddle*, if you're a Pink Floyd freak), filmed beautifully... At one point he's [Roger Waters] banging a massive gong and the sun's coming up in the background. I remember watching and going, "Oh my God, that's amazing, incredible! Then just tried to copy it,' explains Conor. 'And then for some reason I got into bands like Green Day and stuff that was at the complete opposite end of the spectrum, because I hadn't really heard any punk, so I thought they were the first. I hadn't heard the Sex Pistols yet, so I was like, "Oh wow, what's this?" It sounded like the opposite of Pink Floyd.'

At that same time Conor was starting to play in bands with friends. 'There was no music in our school at all, no music class or anything, which was kind of stupid. I was just playing with Dave [David Hedderman] and Pete [Peter Toomey] from the Immediate. The three of us were in school together. Me and Dave played together since we were about twelve. We used to go up to each other's houses a lot and just try to write songs and listen to David Bowie all the time. Dave was a big Bowie freak from very early on, so he used to do crazy things,' says Conor

Surrounded by adventurous, imaginative music like David Bowie and Pink Floyd, Conor's ears were opened to a alternative world of music, a world that was different from what he was hearing on daytime radio, where rules could be broken. 'As long as you just have enough knowledge of them [the rules] then you can walk all over them, trample all over them! That's the thing, *that's* the exciting bit,' says Conor.

'Pete started a band with another fellow in our school, completely separate from me and Dave, and he called his band the Immediate. He asked me to join as a stand-in drummer, while they found a drummer, because I was in another band as well. I started enjoying playing with them and I wrote a song for that band and then I said, "Actually can I sing that?" So Pete was like, "I'll play drums on it then." He'd never played drums before, so he started holding a beat down and that's how the swapping thing began,' explains Conor.

'We never decided to be a band that swapped instruments or anything: it just happened from the first moment we started playing and then we just kept it up and it became central to the live show.'

'We were about sixteen and then Dave joined when we were about seventeen or eighteen, when we were leaving school. It was just a big mash of friends in school and then eventually some people would realise that it wasn't for them and they left. We had another guy called Eoghan O'Reilly who was in the band until about two years before we split. We were just about to record the album when he left the band. I remember being on the phone to the record label going, "I'll record all his bits, let's just do the album!" and they wouldn't. They were like, "No, no, no. You've to find a new member and you've to tour with them and we've to decide if we like you again."'

An old friend, Barra Heavey, joined the Immediate then and they gigged for six months around Dublin to prove themselves fit to their label Fantastic Plastic. 'They were like, "Yeah, OK, it works" and that's when we recorded the album, finally,' says Conor.

Prior to doing the album with Fantastic Plastic, the Immediate had already released a seven-inch single, 'Never Seen', on Fierce Panda. The single was very well received and there was a buzz around the band following their shows in London.

'We recorded it in our house,' reveals Conor. 'It was cool, it was a real little scratchy, DIY, indie thing. I still listen to it sometimes, I dig it out. I actually prefer it to the album because the first release was nice and raw and we left all the mistakes in.'

'There's a programme called Autotune and, you can hear vocals slipping into the right notes and stuff, which is what our producer did when we did the Immediate album. We were like, "Stop tuning our vocals!" Maybe it was needed once or twice (probably) but he did it all over the place. He did a good job, I think he was just doing what needed to be done, for a young band, in the short period of time that he had. We learned a lot.'

'With the Villagers I'm planning on making sure that the recordings are soulful before they're perfect. I want them to be real, something really nice and alive, not something perfect.'

Things had been going well for he Immediate, with sold-out shows in Ireland, a release and a tour on the way in France and a nomination for album of the year for *In Towers and Clouds* at the Choice Music Prize 2007. The announcement that they were breaking up in May 2007 came as a big shock. Industry speculation was that it must have been to do with the difficulties around having three rotating lead singers (egos?) but that wasn't the case.

'It was always going to be tough but that was the thing about that band: we formed in school and we were just having fun. When it got a bit more serious we realised it was not going to work if we tried to make it into a saleable thing. We felt, "We're going to have to mould this into something a bit more commercial or something if it's going to work," and once we did that it would have been a different band anyway, so we ended it. It just felt right to end it.

'I think if we hadn't been getting press we would all have been, "OK, that was fun, let's do something else with our lives now." It *was* fun but Dave wanted to be a painter and he was like, "I've no time to paint at the moment." That's what he is. When someone is what they are, they can't deny it. I know that I'm definitely a musician, because I'll do that if I've a free day, I'll just spend it trying to write something or just making music. We'd been lying to ourselves for the final year, trying to keep it going; it was like a relationship. To everyone else it looked so sudden but to us it felt like a relief.'

'A band is such a claustrophobic thing. The inner dynamic *has* to work or else, no matter how good it's going outside the band, it's not gonna work. It was just over. That's why it was so hard for us to give an explanation, and why we wrote "existential differences!"' laughs Conor

Dave moved to Berlin [to be an artist] so we email each other and if I go to Berlin I'll stay with him. We're just mates from school and for a while we were constantly around each other and now we're not, we just keep in touch. It was kind of natural,' says Conor

'When the band ended I wrote a song the next morning. I got very drunk that night and then I woke up at seven and I went out to the loft and wrote a song. Then Cathy [Davey] called me three days later and I told her the band had split. She was going on tour the week after that and she was like, "Come on tour," and my initial thing was, "No, no, no, it's too soon, it's too soon (again like a relationship)," laughs Conor. 'Then I called her back and went, "What else am I going to do?"'

'I learned so much from her. I had never played in a band with any other musicians, it was really bizarre, the different feels from different musicians. Suddenly I was like, "Oh, things can be done differently!" and realising things about songwriting. It was a really good learning experience playing with her. She comes up with these amazing ideas musically, some great things which I wouldn't have really thought of. I'd come at things from a different angle (and she would say the same thing). It was great to be able to tour, to keep playing music and then when you were free, you were writing. It was ideal,' says Conor

Conor had some songs written (that had never been intended for the Immediate) as well as new songs that he had written while he was playing with Cathy. There was a great deal of anticipation within the music industry around Conor's solo material. What would it be like and when will he release it? The buzz was instant.

'When I put the MySpace up, which I think was October [2008], it was totally on a whim. One night I was like, "Ah, I'm just going to put some demos up!" I made a little bit of artwork, scanned it in; just threw it up,' explains Conor. The first thing was bloggers and stuff and that was straight off, I think Nialler9 and someone else contacted me within a day of putting them up. They must be on the internet constantly, I don't know how they found it even!' says Conor

'I think our first gig was supporting the Chapters,' recalls Conor. Then Vicar Street was our second gig, supporting Bell X1.'

The début release from Villagers was the EP *Hollow Kind* on 6 February 2009. It came out on the small Irish indie label Any Other City, run by James Byrne, who plays drums in Villagers. The artwork was all done by Conor.

'Tommy McLoughlin, who plays guitar in Villagers, recorded that in his home studio in Donegal. It feels really great because it was just the two of us working. It worked really well for that. I play all the instruments on the recordings.'

Hollow Kind was an instant critical hit. Musicians, journalists and fans were in agreement. 'The Meaning of The Ritual' and 'Pieces' were being heard on alternative radio shows across the nation and TV soon joined the list, with an invitation to perform on *The Eleventh Hour* after its release.

Villagers' supports slots were being talked about as they toured with Bell X1 in Ireland and the UK, with the EP being sold in volume after each show. 'It's going really well and the shows we're playing are all being well received,' says Conor

'I was really worried; it was kind of stupid,' he admits.

'One of my main worries when I started was singing really quiet songs in front of people because I had never done it before. I wanted to sing really quiet songs and I was worried people would be just talking all the time, talking over them. I've been realising slowly that people shut up when you genuinely lose yourself in a song on a stage, instead of trying to second-guess what they're thinking or when they're looking at you. If you *really* lose yourself, people can't *not* look at someone who's completely at ease or who's doing something which is really natural to them. I think it was someone from Sonic Youth who said, "People pay to go and see other people believe in themselves on a stage." That's pretty much what showbusiness is. People want to see someone talking for a certain part of them or a certain aspect of them; embodying it physically and in music as well,' says Conor

'I'm really working hard at trying not to be too self-conscious. It's just playing songs in front of people, there's nothing important about it – and it's the most important thing in the world as well. The best way to think is that there's nothing important about it, it's just something natural. It's an extension of talking to someone, so it's just keeping hold of that and trying to maintain

that kind of perspective, not be too serious about anything,' smiles Conor

Things stepped up a gear early on for Villagers, before the EP had even been released, when Paul Wilson from Creative Artists Agency (CAA) came to see them play.

'He's the only one who actually came, travelled to Dublin to see us. Everyone else was like, "Ah, I'll wait till they come to London, they sound all right." He came to the first night in Vicar Street with Bell X1 and then we met him after the show, had a big chat and he was like, "Yeah, I want to be your agent," and I was like, "Cool!" I had a look at his roster and he looks after Antony and the Johnsons, Noah and the Whale, Martha Wainwright, Tracy Chapman – all these diverse but interesting in their own way [artists], the majority of them I was like, "Oh. that's kind of cool, he's got an interesting ear." Then he sent another email saying he was really eager and he loved it and I was like, "Yeah, cool, let's do it!"'

With an agent in place, Conor had to think about how to release Villagers' first album. To sign or not to sign. Having worked with a couple of independent labels with the Immediate, Conor knew what questions to ask and what he wanted for his new project. He did not jump at the first offer.

Numerous label and publishing deals were on the table over the summer of 2009. Having weighed up the various options, Conor chose the independent label, Double Six Records, a Domino label. He also signed a publishing deal with Domino Publishing. The announcement came with word of his final release on *Any Other City*, a seven-inch vinyl single 'On A Sunlit Stage' and an Irish tour in October.

With his label and publishing in place, Conor is ready to record. 'I should have the album finished by the end of the year,' says Conor. 'I was thinking of maybe getting the band down for a couple

of things but for the most part it'll be just me and Tommy working for a month. We're going to try and keep it short and sweet but also kind of epic. I think eleven is a nice number of songs for an album. I'm going to try and do all the artwork, which takes ages, and we're going to try and make a video as well…I'm going to have to get my boots on!'

In under a year Conor has found management, an agent, a publisher and a label for Villagers. With the début album nearly ready, one wonders what he hopes for next? 'I'd love to headline Vicar Street with this band because I think it'd just be the best gig ever. It's my favourite venue maybe in Ireland.'

'I just want to play to as many people as possible. If nothing came of it I'd still be doing it in my bedroom, I'd be writing stuff and not that whole thing of, "it's a bonus if people listen to it," but I get a massive rush when people finally hear something you've been keeping to yourself for a year or whatever. The main thing for me, in my head, is that I want to be able to do it in different countries, I want to be able to travel.

'I remember something someone told me recently. A very reputable musician who has toured for his whole life told me that you only really find out if your songs have legs if they really strike people in another culture or with another language. That's the real litmus test and I still have never really got the chance to do that. I think that when you write songs, when you've written songs for a long time, this thing takes over. That's the next step and it's obvious that you need to get there, to that next step, or else it'll feel like you're stuck. I need to bring it further afield. That's our next thing. I'm quietly confident we're going to do that!'

So are we.

Villagers highly anticipated, début full-length is expected on Double Six in early 2010.

The following is a snapshot of some of the many Irish artists being talked about, played and filling venues around the country.

Hot List

▲   **And So I Watch You From Afar**   ▼   **The Ambience Affair**

IN BLOOM - HOT LIST

The Ambience Affair

www.myspace.com/theambienceaffair

The Ambience Affair comprises vocalist/guitarist Jamie Clarke and drummer Marc Gallagher. Jamie had been playing and writing solo until he met Marc in the music shop they both work in. Marc came to one of his gigs and thy decided to form a band. *Fragile Things*, their début EP, was recorded in three days and had a limited first print of 100 hand-made copies which sold out (as did the second print). *Fragile Things* showcased haunting, urgent, beautiful songs from a young band with time and talent on their side. The Ambience Affair's second EP is due out in January 2010 on Indiecater Records. They have supported Villagers, Fight Like Apes and Ham Sandwich, amongst others.

And So I Watch You From Afar

www.myspace.com/andsoiwatchyoufromafar

And So I Watch You From Afar is the four-piece instrumental band from Belfast that has been causing a massive media stir over the past year. The band formed in 2006 and since then has toured constantly throughout Ireland and the UK. Critics appeared unanimous in their praise for their début album *This Is Our Machine and Nothing Can Stop It* (including four Ks in Kerrang! and 10/10 from BBC Radio One) when it was released on Smalltown America in March 2009, but it is their live shows that continue to evoke the biggest reactions and the highest praise. Dark, epic and beautiful, And So I Watch You from Afar's songs, 'A Little Solidarity Goes A Long Way' and 'Set Guitars to Kill', have had extensive alternative radio play. In 2009 they played Mandela Hall, Oxegen, Glasgowbury, the Academy 2 and they play their largest headline to date in December: Belfast's Ulster Hall.

▲ The Chakras ▼ The Angel Pier

IN BLOOM - HOT LIST

The Angel Pier

www.myspace.com/angelpier
www.angelpier.com

The Angel Pier is a four-piece – Darragh Nolan, Mark Colbert, Luke Paluch, and Vinny Redmond – based in Dublin. They have released two EPs and a 7". The début EP, *Bullet Holes & Broken Sectors*, came out in 2007, followed by *Sacrifice EP* in 2008. They started 2009 with a show in Whelans, followed by the headline spot on the 'Best Of' IMRO Showcase Tour' gig at the Village in May and performances at Oxegen in July on the New Band Stage. They released a limited edition 7" 'Belong'/Align The Seas', followed by performances at Castlepalooza in August and HWCH in October. The sad beauty and driving melody of their music has won the band critical praise and alternative radio play. They have been recording with Jimmy Eadie and hope to release their début album at the end of 2009, with more touring planned for 2010.

The Chakras

www.myspace.com/thechakras
www.thechakras.co.uk

A buzz had started to build around the Chakras on the strength of their self-released EP, *Build Me a Swan*. They were 'featured artist' on MySpace, which is where David Boyd (MD of Flock Music, former MD Hut Recordings and A&R for Virgin Records) heard them. He approached them and became their manager. They went into studio with Chris Potter [The Verve, Urban Hymns] to record a track for digital release – 'We the People', with a new line-up and drummer. The next nine months were spent writing and recording – when they could afford to – with producer Jaz Rogers in Dublin's Cauldron Studios. The album is recorded and ready to be mixed. Universal Ireland got in touch, loved it and decided to release 'Build Me a Swan' as a digital single. It was mixed by Declan Gaffney [U2 No Line on the Horizon] in Grouse Lodge Studios and came out on Universal Records on 25 September 2009. A series of tour dates followed in October. With experienced management and a good agent [CAA], the Chakras are very well placed to go big. They are currently in talks with major labels in the UK to release their début album in 2010.

▲ Cowboy X ▼ Dark Room Notes

IN BLOOM - HOT LIST

Cowboy X

www.myspace.com/cowboyxmusic

The producing and songwriting duo, John Hanley and David Grealy, had been playing music together for years. They had more or less written what would later become their début album, *Who Are These People?*, but were not happy with their own voices on it – they wanted a female voice. John met Karen McCartney in 2005 in Temple Lane Studios while working on a session and he asked her if she could sing. Karen thought she was auditioning for backing vocals but her voice was exactly what they were looking for in a lead. The three finished the album together with Karen rewriting as needed. They were later joined by Wayne Gibson on bass. *Who Are These People?* was released in June 2006 on their own-label Actual Size Records and featured the 1980s-tinged, electro-pop radio hit 'Gabbi'. Working full-time and recording on the side, Cowboy X released the single 'Japanese Toy' with a video to accompany it in the summer of 2008 and played Electric Picnic. The single 'Break Me' followed in early 2009, receiving extensive alternative radio play and winning them many new fans. A 4-track EP, *Analogue Droids*, was released in October 2009 with a launch show in Whelans. 'Analogue Droids' is the third single from their forthcoming, second studio album, *Meant to Be Machines*, which is due out in 2010.
(Read the interview with Cowboy X on www.inbloom.ie.)

Dark Room Notes

www.myspace.com/darkroomnotesireland

Ronan Gaughan and Ruairi Ferrie are childhood friends from Galway. They met Aaran Murphy and Darragh Shanahan in Dublin, where Dark Room Notes were formed. In April 2007 they released their single, 'Love Like Nicotine', on the indie label Gonzo Records. Their début EP, *Dead Start Program,* followed in October 2007, garnering the band large amounts of positive press. Dark Room Notes' cool elctro-rock/synth pop sound and stylish live shows quickly won them fans up and down the country. Radio play and television appearances soon followed, including a now legendary acoustic performance, 'Shake Shake My Ceiling', on *Other Voices*. *We Love You Dark Matter*, their début full-length, was released in April 2009, featuring the singles 'Let's Light Fires' and 'This Hot Heat'. Dark Room Notes put equal effort into the visual side of the band, with stunning videos for their songs. In October, 2009 Dark Room Notes signed to the Berlin/London label BBE. Their début album *We Love You Dark Matter* will receive a worldwide release in 2010 with BBE and the band are set to tour in the UK, Europe, US and Japan.
(Read the interview with Ronan Gaughan and Ruairi Ferrie on www.inbloom.ie)

▲ Director ▼ Dirty Epics

IN BLOOM - HOT LIST

Director

www.myspace.com/directormusic
Website: www.directormusic.com

Director are: Eoin Aherne, Rowan Averill, Shea Lawlor and Michael Moloney.

Their début album, *We Thrive On Big Cities*, reached Number 2 in the Irish charts, spending weeks in the Top Thirty and going platinum in the process. It was shortlisted for the Choice Music Prize Irish Album of the Year 2006. In 2007 Director won a Meteor Award for Best New Irish Act. They have done numerous high-profile support slots and sold-out tours of Ireland and have headlined shows in the Ambassador and the Olympia. They have played the main stage at Oxegen and the Trinity Ball.

Director took the independent route for their second album, *I'll Wait For Sound*, releasing it on their own Crapshoot Economics label in May 2009. It was preceded by the single 'Sing It Without A Tune'. Produced by Brad Wood, this showcased a harder, more confident sound from the band, winning great reviews from the critics. 'Moment To Moment' was the second single released from the album, followed by 'Don't Think I'll Know' in October. Director released *I'll Wait For Sound* in the UK through ADA Global in September 2009. They did an extensive Irish tour throughout October and November 2009.
(Read the interview with Director on www.inbloom.ie.)

Dirty Epics

www.myspace.com/dirtyepics

Dirty Epics have a punk-influenced, dirty-pop sound. Comprising Sarah Jane Wai O'Flynn (SJ Wai), Cormac Farrell, Richie Power and Alan Delaney from Wicklow, Dirty Epics have released a series of popular singles. They have worked hard over the past few years and hive gigged regularly. Their début album, *Straight In No Kissing*, produced by Dave Morgan and Gareth Mannix, was released in October 2008. 'The Cure', 'Way Too Pretty', 'We're Coming Up' and 'Pony' all received radio play and had videos created for them. Dirty Epics came to greater national attention through the RTE television programme, *The Raw Sessions*, and have played Oxegen, Indie-pendence, and HWCH.

▲ **Fighting with Wire** ▼ **General Fiasco**

IN BLOOM - HOT LIST

Fighting with Wire

www.myspace.com/fightingwithwire
www.fightingwithwire.co.uk

Fighting with Wire began in 2003, the new project of guitarist Cahir O'Doherty (Jetplane Landing and Clearshot) and drummer Craig McKean (Clearshot). Jamie King then joined and they have toured the UK and Ireland constantly over the last few years. Fighting with Wire have developed a reputation for their ferocious live shows, playing with Biffy Clyro, Seafood and Future of the Left. They released a number of limited-edition DIY singles before releasing their début proper, *Man Vs Monster*, in March 2008. *Man Vs Monster* featured the singles 'Everyone Needs a Nemesis' and 'All For Nothing'. Their third single, 'Sugar', was a huge radio hit in the UK and Ireland with crossover radio play and alternative radio playlisting. Fighting With Wire are signed to Atlantic Records but have maintained their indie roots and early DIY ethic by continuing to release their music through Derry-based label Small Town America in the UK and Ireland. They recorded their second album in America in the autumn of 2009, with the first single due for release in early 2010.

General Fiasco

www.myspace.com/general fiasco

Brothers Owen and Enda Strathern met Stephen 'Leaky' Leacock in school. They formed General Fiasco in 2007 and have since been on endless tours of the UK and Ireland. 7' single, 'Rebel Get By', was released by indie label Another Music = Another Kitchen in November 2008 and picked up high-profile Irish and UK radio play including the BBC and XFM. 'Something Sometime' was released on their own label in March 2009 and had the honour of being Zane Lowe's 'Hottest Record In the World'. General Fiasco then signed a deal with Infectious Records and 'We Are the Foolish' was their début single on the label, released on 12 October 2009. They have played the Reading and Leeds Festivals, Electric Proms, Download, Glastonbury and Oxegen. They did their own headline tour, followed by a support tour with the Enemy, throughout the autumn of 2009. General Fiasco's début album is due for release in early 2010.

▲ **Giveamanakick** ▼ **Halves**

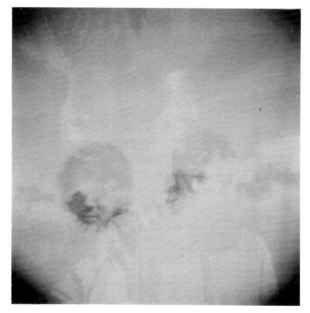

IN BLOOM - HOT LIST

Giveamanakick (RIP)

www.myspace.com/giveamanakick

(steveamanakick and giveamanakeith = giveamanakick) Limerick boys Steve Ryan and Keith Lawler are the rock dynamo that was Giveamanakick (GAMAK). They released three albums on the Limerick-based indie label, Out On A Limb Records: *Is It OK To Be Loud, Jesus?*, *We Are the Way Forward* and *Welcome to the Cusp*. GAMAK played with Yeah Yeah Yeahs, the Rapture, Dinosaur Jr, Deftones, Presidents of the United States of America, Electric 6, the Icarus Line and the Undertones. They also played numerous festivals across Ireland and Europe, including Electric Picnic and Reeperbahn in Germany. Their third album, *Welcome to the Cusp,* saw GAMAK head into more melodic, radio-friendly territory than in their previous two albums, with lead single, 'Borrowed Time', receiving alternative radio play immediately on its release. GAMAK played CMJ in New York in November 2008, to rave reviews, and Canadian Music Week in March 2009. The release of the second single from *Welcome to the Cusp*, 'Brittle Bones', was followed by an acoustic Irish tour throughout March and April.

On 16 August 2009 the respected duo announced that, after seven years and three albums, they would be winding up the band through a video posted on their site. The press statement said 'Giveamanakick was always meant to make a certain kind of impact. We feel we've made that impact now, and we are both happy to move on.' A farewell tour was announced for November-December 2009 with previously unreleased, limited-edition and live material available for fans at the shows. (Read the interview with Steve and Keith on www.inbloom.ie.)

Halves

www.myspace.com/ahomeforhalves

Halves are Brian Cash, Elis Czerniak, Tim Czerniak and Dave Scanlon. Described mainly as post-rock, they use a huge range of instruments to create their haunting sound: electric guitars, bass, drumkit, piano, electric violin, viola, glockenspiel, accordian, synth, vocoder, reed organ, melodica, sleigh bells, bell chorus, omnichord, saw, laptops, loop samplers, and various effects.

The band have released two EPs, *Halves* and *Haunt Me When I'm Drowsy* (2008). They then released a limited-edition single, 'Blood Branches', in March 2009 on a split 7" with the band Subplots. Halves have played Oxegen, Electric Picnic, Hard Working Class Heroes, the IMRO Showcase Tour, London Calling, Eurosonic and Canadian Music Week. They have supported British Sea Power, 65daysofstatic, Bell X1 and Cathy Davey. Their gig on 19 June 2009 was Dave's last with Halves, but they hoped to have him around for some of the recording of their début full-length album. They started this in August, with Efrim Menuck of Godspeed You! Black Emperor in Montreal.

▲ Ham Sandwich ▼ Heathers

IN BLOOM - HOT LIST

Ham Sandwich

www.myspace.com/eathamsandwich

Ham Sandwich are Niamh Farrell, Podge McNamee, John Moore and friends Ollie Murphy and Darcy from Kells, County Meath. They released their début single, 'Sad Songs', in 2005, 'St Christopher' in 2006 and 'Click…Click… Boom!' in 2007. 'Click… Click… Boom!' was a huge radio hit and crowd favourite, showing a sexier side to the band. Ham Sandwich won Hope for 2008 at the Meteor Ireland Music Awards on 15 February 2008, the same day they self-released their début album, *Carry the Meek*, on Route 109 Records. They released further singles and did headline shows before they turned their attention to writing their second album. Great music, regular touring, confetti-drenched shows and a distinctive name has Ham Sandwich high in public consciousness in Ireland. Their second album is nearly finished and is due for release in 2010.
(Read the full interview with Niamh Farrell on www.inbloom.ie.)

Heathers

www.myspace.com/heatherswhatsyourdamage

Heathers are twin sisters Ellie and Louise MacNamara from Dublin. Their name comes from the 1980s cult film *Heathers* (starring Christian Slater and Winona Ryder). The title of their single, 'What's Your Damage', is also a quote from the film. They were only eighteen when their début album, *Here, Not There,* was released. *Here, Not There* was released as a joint release on Hide Away Records (Ireland) and Plan-it-x Records (USA) on 23 May 2008. It was preceded by the single 'Remember When'. With only Louise's guitar to accompany them, their distinct, powerful voices and striking harmonies drew immediate comparisons to the Indigo Girls and Canadian sisters Tegan and Sara. The critics understandably loved them. Heathers spent most of 2008 touring North America and Ireland. They played the CMJ festival in New York, and Canadian Music Week in Toronto and supported Kimya Dawson (Juno, Moldy Peaches) and Ghost Mice. They Played the new band stage at Oxegen and did a headline show in the Project Arts Centre in Dublin in October 2009. Fans await their new material.,

Home Star Runner

www.myspace.com/homestarrunner

Home Star Runner is pop punk band from Dunboyne, County Meath, with a charismatic front man and high- energy performances. Their popularity and American sound have led to high-profile supports slots to Paramore, Elliot Minor and New Found Glory. With their début album, *Kill the Messenger*, and a fresh EP, *All Systems Are Failing*, behind them, Home Star Runner packed the tent at Oxegen 2009, proving just how big their fan base has become.

▲ Panama Kings   ▼ Oliver Cole

IN BLOOM - HOT LIST

The Minutes

www.myspace.com/theminutesireland

Dublin band, the Minutes, stand out for their great melodies and harmonies. They released their first single, 'Ukraine', in 2007. It was an instant hit with DJs for its infectious chorus and melodic indie pop sound. It was followed by 'Harmonic' in 2008. Rather than rush into an album, the Minutes chose to hone their live sound instead, gigging constantly and doing a residency upstairs in Whelans.

The band spent the summer of 2008 doing 'Gigs in Your Gaff' shows – an open call for people to contact them to come to their house to play a show. 'Black Keys', released in the summer of 2009, was the first sign of their new sound. The Minutes have toured with and supported Albert Hammond Jnr (The Strokes), The Pigeon Detectives, The Von Bondies, Fountains Of Wayne and Supergrass.

The band did a small tour of North America with shows in NYC, Toronto (CMW 2009) and Boston. They returned to New York in October 2009 for CMJ, with plans to work with producer Gareth Mannix on their début album.

Oliver Cole

www.myspace.com/olivercole

Ollie Cole was the lead singer of Turn, one of Ireland great rock bands. Saddened by their break-up, fans waited to hear if Ollie would continue to write and start another project. Solo material was being much talked about in music circles and then, in 2008, a few demos were posted on his website for fans to hear. Ollie recorded his début solo album, *We Albatri*, in Germany with Ciaran Bradshaw in the summer of 2008. Initially he planned an independent release in May of 2009, but word spread of its infectious charm and EMI Ireland stepped in. The three-song EP *What Will You Do?* was released on EMI Ireland on 2 October 2009, followed by an Irish tour. Ollie writes vulnerable, alternative love songs and catchy indie pop gems: songs with stories that ooze melody and keep a hint of his natural Kells accent. His full-length solo début, *We Albatri*, will be released on EMI in February 2010.

Panama Kings

www.myspace.com/panamakings

Belfast's Panama Kings won the JD Unsigned band competition in 2008. Their début EP, *Young Blood*, won over the press and received extensive alternative radio support throughout Ireland and the UK. Signed to indie label No Dancing, they supported Eagles Of Death Metal, The Virgins and Duke Special. Their single, 'Golden Recruit', released on Broken Sound in May 2009, was another alternative radio hit. October saw them headline the Mandela Hall and touring the UK with Ash. With labels knocking at their door, everything seems to be heading in the right direction for Panama Kings.

▲ R.S.A.G. ▼ The Rags

IN BLOOM - HOT LIST

The Rags

www.myspace.com/therags

Dublin indie rock six-piece, the Rags, have released two successful EPs and three singles. Their début EP, *Me and the Moon*, was released in April 2004, recorded by Ciaran Bradshaw. The Rag's next EP, *Monsters and I*, was released in February 2005, winning them alternative radio play for 'Strawberry Bed' and 'Monsters and I'. The single 'Razors & Ropes' followed in July 2006. They were busy gigging the alternative venues to growing and enthusiastic crowds, when 'Monsters and I' was used on a TV commercial for soup in Ireland. The Rags hit mainstream awareness immediately and the song was re-released as a single and added to daytime radio playlists. They have played Electric Picnic and HWCH and supported Aslan, Brendan Benson and the Rakes. After a long absence from the live scene, the Rags returned with a digital single, 'A Mirror to a Woman (Is a Bullet in a Gun)', on 25 Sept 2009 (Grand Cake Records), followed by a national tour in October 2009. The band's long-awaited début album, *A National Light,* is due for release in March 2010.

R.S.A.G.

www.myspace.com/rarelyseenaboveground
www.rsagmusic.com

R.S.A.G. (or Rarely Seen Above Ground) is multi-instrumentalist and drumming wonderboy Jeremy Hickey from Kilkenny. Jeremy wows audiences with his live show, performed solo with synched backing tracks and recorded images of him playing the other instruments on a screen behind him. He performed, wrote, produced and mixed his self-titled début, *Rarely Seen Above Ground*. R.S.A.G.'s second album, *Organic Sampler* (produced, arranged, composed and performed by Hickey), was released on Psychonavigation Records in 2008 to rave reviews. *Organic Sampler* was shortlisted for the Choice Music Prize Irish Album of the Year 2008. In 2009 Hickey was a finalist in the TV music show, *The Raw Sessions*, toured nationally, played Oxegen and Electric Picnic and started work on his third album (due for release in 2010).
(Read the interview with Jeremy Hickey on www.inbloom.ie.)

▲ Talulah Does the Hula   ▼   Yes Cadets

IN BLOOM - HOT LIST

Talulah Does the Hula

www.myspace.com/talulahdoesthehula

Talulah Does the Hula (TDTH) is the Dublin indie-pop quintet made up of ex-members of the Chalets and Neosupervital. Lauren, Jessie, Caoimhe, Paula and Mike came together, inspired by retro sounds from the Shangri-Las to the Cars.

Gigs in Crawdaddy and supports around the country had people talking not only about their fantastic style but their great harmonies and sexy tunes. TDTH released their début double-A side 'Bad Boyfriend'/'Those Girls' on 26 June 2009 to overwhelmingly positive reviews. The radio loved it, spreading word of their vocal charms. More gigs and touring followed. They have done support slots to Adam Green and the Cribs and played HWCH in October. Expect a busy and high-profile 2010.

Yes Cadets

www.myspace.com/yescadets
www.yescadets.com

Yes Cadets were formed in Belfast over the summer of 2008, through a mutual love of Canadian indie music. Their electro pop/art-rock style appealed to national radio DJs, with radio play for their demo 'Charm Offensive'. They played at Oxegen and Glastonbury and have done numerous support shows. The four-piece have been generally causing a stir since releasing their début single, 'Canada', at the beginning of September 2009. Yes Cadets then released their first self-titled EP, *Yes Cadets*, on 25 October 2009. The release was followed by a UK and Irish tour throughout October and November 2009. 2010 is certain to be active.

TRACKLISTING